Co-op management and employment

John Berry and Mark Roberts

Berry, John, 19—
    Co-op management and employment.— (Running a workers co-op,
ISSN 0265–5659; 1)
    1. Employee ownership—Great Britain
    2. Employees' representation in management—Great Britain
    I. Title   II. Roberts, Mark, 19—
    III. Series
    334'.6'0941   HD5660.G7

    ISBN 0–946776–04–0

First published in February 1984 by ICOM Co-Publications
7 Bradbury Street, London N16

ISBN 0 946776 04 0

Cover design by Len Breen
Typeset and printed by Calvert's Press Ltd, 55 Mount Pleasant,
London WC1X 0AE.

Contents

Introduction

This handbook is primarily addressed to members of small to medium sized workers co-ops which make up the majority of co-ops in Britain today. The authors' experience—both in working in co-ops and in co-operative development work—has been in these sorts of co-ops. However, many of the points made in the handbook will also apply to larger co-ops.

It is important first of all to define what is meant by a 'workers co-operative'. This is an issue on which there is at present some debate. However, for the purposes of this handbook, when we talk about a workers co-op we mean:

- it is registered under the Industrial and Provident Societies Acts or the Companies Acts and therefore has a legal personality, limited liability and its worker members are employees
- ownership is exercised collectively rather than individually
- if membership is not confined solely to the workforce, then at least eighty per cent of the members are employees
- the dissolution clause in the rules does not allow members to benefit individually
- it is based on co-operative principles as laid down by the International Co-operative Alliance

Generally speaking, this will mean co-operatives registered under the model rules of the Industrial Common Ownership Movement and over ninety per cent of workers co-ops in Britain are registered in this way.

Workers in organisations which are not owned and controlled by their employees should be very wary of some of the working practices outlined in this handbook. It is essential that the responsibilities of running a workers co-operative go hand in hand with control of the assets and thus the rewards. Workers should not allow such responsibilities to be forced upon them unless they genuinely control the enterprise they work in.

Although some of the matters discussed in the handbook apply to all co-operatives because they are legal duties—particularly in the section on employment—we do not wish to lay down a blueprint for the organisation of all co-ops. It is entirely up to the working members to decide how they want to organise their own co-op in terms both of ideals and day to day practice. Their decision will obviously be affected by the size and type of business the co-operative is running, but the rights of workers in a co-operative mean they can adopt any structure they wish—even a traditional management structure. However, if they do adopt a traditional structure, this may affect their ability to act as a true co-operative.

Internal organisation on co-operative lines is the *sine qua non* of co-op firms. Without it, co-ops are merely small companies run not by their workforce but by their managers or by external forces. Yet the achievement of a real and effective internal co-operative organisation depends on the profitability of the enterprise. Co-operative elements in an unprofitable enterprise can be stifled by external forces or by managers pleading poverty. The modern retail co-operative movement, which in comparison to its history is now democratically moribund, bears witness to this dilution of co-operative control. External forces will always have a bearing on the potential for co-operation and this should be remembered when planning organisational structures.

Internal organisation is the nuts and bolts of running your co-operative as a co-operative. How you make your decisions, how you treat yourselves as employees, how you run your meetings and how you relate to the outside world are all vitally important to the co-operative working as a co-operative.

There are no hard and fast rules to follow when deciding how to organise your co-op. You should, however, give careful consideration to the basic areas of

- rules and secondary rules
- decision making systems
- running meetings
- internal relations
- financial information for co-op members
- community involvement
- conditions of employment

We will now go on to look at each of these areas in turn.

Rules and secondary rules

The system of internal organisation in any co-operative is based on the rules or memorandum and articles of association adopted. In some cases the constitution of the co-operative will be tailor-made in which case many aspects of the system of organisation decided upon would be incorporated into it. However most new co-operatives choose to register under standard model rules or memorandum and articles which provide a simple and basic framework to build the co-operative's organisation on. In order to establish the organisation of a co-operative to fit in with these rules, it is important first of all to digest them carefully. For instance, some model rules require the co-op to have a manager. This has fundamental implications for decision making within the co-op and because it is in the rules, it cannot be ignored.

Many members however do not read the rules—even though they should be issued with a set when they become members—and quite often members have little interest in the pursuance of legal requirements. This does put a big responsibility on the secretary of the co-operative to ensure that the co-operative stays within its rules or changes them. Equally, the whole group has a responsibility to work at co-operation even though members may not be aware of the finer legal points. Individual members must work at co-operation and democracy in the workplace. It doesn't simply happen because you have a constitution and rules. Paying lip service to the ideals of co-operation without actually putting them into practice is too common a fault among worker co-operatives. Working at decision making processes to improve them, at involving all of the workforce and at the spreading of information are all vital ingredients in the success of a co-operative.

Having established the legal constitution of the co-operative whether by means of model rules or by a tailor-made constitution, it is important to examine the provisions within those rules for the internal organisation of the co-operative. Thus the rules or articles of association may stipulate the type or composition of the management committee of the co-operative, the number and remit of designated posts such as secretary and treasurer and the type of information that is required and the decisions that have to be made, for example, on the distribution of profits and the appointment of auditors. In most cases these rules are not cast in tablets of stone but will normally require at least a three quarters majority for change and then become valid only when registered with the Registrar of Friendly Societies or Companies House. The registrar does have the power to refuse changes in rules particularly those which affect the nature of the co-op as a co-op and which take it outside the guidelines the registrar has outlined.

The rules or articles of association provide the framework for the working of the co-operative. In most cases this framework does not go into much detail and provides only a basic outline for co-operative management. For this reason co-operatives often add what are known as 'secondary rules' to the co-op which provide a more detailed plan of organisation. These rules do not necessarily have to be registered with the registrar. Indeed a fee would be payable for such an alteration to the primary rules. The rules can be recorded in a separate document which has been agreed by the co-op in a meeting or they can be recorded as they come up at meetings in the minutes of those meetings. These rules can be changed and new ones agreed by either a simple majority or preferably a three quarters majority. These secondary rules may explore any area of organisation but here are some examples.

Job rotation and transfer

One common example of a secondary rule might be the institution of a system of job rotation within a co-operative. Thus the rule might state

> *there are ten different job areas within the co-operative. Each worker will change to a different job area each month according to the timetable drawn up from time to time by the co-operative*

The idea behind such a rule is to spread knowledge of and skills in all aspects of the business so that all members can take a full and equal part in the running of the enterprise and individuals can develop their own personal expertise. The attractions of such a scheme are obvious. There is the possibility of a far more varied working life, the likelihood of more informed decision making and a certain degree of satisfaction in challenging traditional divisions of labour. However, the feasibility of such schemes varies with the type of people involved and the type of firm that the co-op is.

In enterprises such as shops, for example, the possibilities of job rotation are much greater than in other enterprises. Workers can take responsibility for a number of tasks in the shop such as ordering, bookkeeping and serving and easily change from one task to the other. A high level of training is not required in any of these areas and thus a group of relatively unskilled workers could rotate the jobs quite adequately. In other co-operatives, a division of labour between different skill areas may well be necessary because of the extended training or particular attributes required for the job. This may obviate job rotation. In more complicated production processes, the need for specific skills in specific jobs becomes more apparent.

Job rotation can have disadvantages. Firstly, because different workers will be carrying out tasks at different times, the quality of the work is likely to vary from one month to the next. This can be confusing for outside customers and suppliers and can have a detrimental effect on the success of the business. Secondly, instead of giving job satisfaction to co-op members, the rotation system might result in co-op members having to do work that they do not particularly like. Lastly, the fact that workers vary in the quality of their work and their interest in doing it results in those who are better at specific tasks having to clear up the mess left by the previous person. This is particularly true in the case of bookkeeping where some members might well have complete mental blocks which, although important to overcome, might result in the next worker having to work overtime to resolve intractable arithmetical problems in the books.

Many co-ops maintain that job rotation, although it might be inefficient in business terms, is an important part of viewing work in a completely new light and that the financial disincentives involved are not sufficient to outweigh the value of the learning process.

In a co-operative firm where it seems more sensible not to have job rotation, consideration ought to be given to other ways of breaking down traditional modes of working. One method is to have a form of job transfer which allows workers to change the work that they do in an orderly and planned way. Individual workers would apply to the co-op meeting or decision making body for transfer to another job function. They would have to give a reasonable period for the plan to be executed and it would depend greatly on a suitable vacancy arising. It would obviously be easier in a larger co-op where more vacancies are continually arising. The worker will probably need to be trained in the new skill area and consideration must also be given to having a probationary period for that worker (not for membership of the co-op) to ensure that if the skills are not picked up, then the member has to return to the old job or a new one as determined by the co-op.

The advantage of this scheme is that it maintains a high level of continuity but at the same time ensures skill sharing and knowledge distribution and flexibility of co-op organisation. The disadvantage is that the management of such a scheme would be relatively complicated.

There is an enormous amount of administrative and co-ordination work in any business. It is entirely possible that instead of placing all the responsibility for administrative tasks in the hands of one or two people, specific jobs could be done by other members of the co-operative. For instance, certain discrete tasks such as PAYE, bookkeeping or stock control could be done by shop floor workers if it was felt to be necessary to involve as many people as possible in the co-operative's management functions. This is a way of demystifying management without devaluing it as a vital ingredient in successful business practice. Other work such as sales, customer relations, production management, financial management etc are more difficult to share and may have to be performed by managers/co-ordinators.

Wage structure

Another example of a secondary rule is the organisation of a wage structure within a co-operative. In many co-operatives wages are not based on the market rates for the particular job skill. Jobs that would be lower paid in the outside world tend to be higher paid in co-ops and quite often jobs that command a higher premium in the market place are paid at a lower rate. The latter is obviously a serious disadvantage in co-ops as key workers would be unlikely to stay for a long period if their main reason for working was money. In most co-ops secondary rules provide for equal wages:

> *all workers shall be paid at the same hourly rate whatever their job within the co-operative*

Some co-ops feel that this does not adequately meet the needs of co-operators and have developed rules which provide for those who have children or other dependants:

> *payment of wages beyond the basic wages will be dependent on need as determined by the co-operative*

Other co-ops are concerned about the turnover in key personnel that can occur if equal wages are the rule and have adopted a system of increments or length of service pay:

> *for every year of service a member of the co-operative shall have her/ his salary increased by the sum of £500*

This certainly reduces the problems of staff turnover but perhaps there should be an agreed limit both to avoid creating too great a differential between the highest paid and the lowest and to ensure that it does not eventually become too great a drain on the co-operative's resources.

In yet other a co-ops, provision is made in the secondary rules for the differential between wages to be limited. Thus, for instance, in the Mondragon co-ops in Spain, the highest wage differs by a factor of three from the lowest wage. These co-ops have however experienced some difficulties in recruiting staff at the top end, particularly doctors.

In most co-operatives, apprentices or trainees are paid at a lower rate than the trained workers on the basis that the trainees' lack of productivity will have to be borne by other members of the co-op and that paying the full wage might well put too great a strain on the individuals concerned or indeed on the co-operative's finances as a whole.

Overtime and time off in lieu

Another area where secondary rules have to be developed is in relation to overtime, time off in lieu and the ability of members to earn more from the co-operative when they wish to. Examples of secondary rules here include:

a full time worker shall work for thirty-five hours in any given week. Any extra time worked shall be taken as time off in lieu rather than as paid overtime

no member shall exceed thirty-five hours time off in lieu

holidays and time off in lieu must be agreed by the co-operative before they are taken

if members wish to earn more than the standard basic wage they may apply to the co-operative to work longer hours

if members work more than thirty-five hours in excess of their basic working time, they may be paid at a rate equivalent to half the normal hourly rate for those hours in excess of the thirty-five hours time off in lieu

members shall be paid overtime at the rate of the normal hourly wage

The above examples show what a complex area this is. Each co-operative must work out what method best suits it and its workers.

Sometimes workers want to earn more money for their own personal needs. This must be recognised, although the worker must also recognise that a full week's work must be put in before extra earnings are justified. The method by which hours are measured must be carefully planned as well. There is unlikely to be a foreman who can check on these things so self-regulation must be the co-operative way. Some co-ops have a clocking-in book in which individuals record time of arrival, time of leaving, lunch taken, hours worked and excess hours. It is important that members regulate themselves and point out to others where they are falling down or abusing the system. Again there a responsibility on all members to work at co-operation.

The decision whether to pay overtime or give time off in lieu must depend on the value placed on the particular time worked by the workers concerned. Some members actually like working on a Sunday and if so, it perhaps does not warrant a special rate of pay. Indeed there is a danger that too much extra payment for overtime can be detrimental to the co-operative as a whole while benefiting individuals considerably. A balanced approach is necessary here to prevent either the collective or the individual suffering.

Probationary periods

Most co-operatives institute secondary rules concerning the taking on of new members and the type and length of probationary period that workers are required to fulfil:

workers must undergo a probationary period of at least six months before being eligible for membership of the co-operative

It should be made clear to new employees as they are taken on what the rules on membership of the co-operative are. For example, will they be measured for membership on the basis of their production skills or their commitment to the co-operative as well? Will they be present when the decision to take them on as members is made, how often can membership be refused to an applicant, does a worker have to apply for membership to ensure complete membership, what percentage of the eligible workforce must be members and should managers be allowed into membership?

Part-time workers present a different problem. Some co-operatives require part-timers to serve a probationary period in proportion to the full-timers' week. Casual workers—ie individuals who work very irregularly for the co-operative or for a short period only—are not normally considered for membership. It may make sense for those workers doing less than ten hours work a week not to be eligible for membership. Probationary periods should not be too long, but might be determined by the level of skill required by the job. Normally they do not exceed a year.

Transfer to full membership should be treated seriously. On becoming a member, workers take on an equal legal responsibility for the co-operative. Issuing a membership or share certificate and a copy of the rules may have the effect of making this clear.

One of the other important areas where many co-operatives develop detailed secondary rules is in relation to contracts of employment, dispute and grievance procedures etc. This is covered in detail in the section on employment.

Decision making

All businesses have to be managed well if they are to be commercially successful. Defining management is not easy but one definition might be 'the organisation of other people's activities to maximise the achievement of set targets'. Thus in a normal capitalist firm, the following hierarchical structure would be adopted:

Shareholders/Board of directors who determine policy targets and distribute the profits

Management who get things done through other people (both workers and outside agents) in order to maximise profits

Workers who take orders from management to produce goods for sale

Co-operatives do not of course fit into this simple structure. However, each co-op must decide whether its members are going to take over the functions of both the shareholders/board of directors and the management. In most small co-ops, members will wish to carry out management tasks as well as exercising ownership but may eventually choose to hire a manager.

However much responsibility is vested outside the control of the whole workforce, the essential questions are: how are decisions made and who makes them? Do you need managers? Is self management the central core of co-operatives or is it collective ownership? Or is accountability for decision making as far as it is necessary to go?

Efficient decision making is essential within any business enterprise. Involvement in decision making is essential in any co-operative enterprise. The interface between these two premises is sometimes conflict, sometimes harmony, but is the nub of the question when considering the internal management structures of co-operatives.

The type of decision making structure will vary in each co-operative because of the type of people within the co-op; the product or service of the co-operative; and the size of the co-operative.

Type of people

Co-operators come from a wide variety of backgrounds. Some may have come to co-ops because they were born in an area where many co-ops trade, some because they have been involved in business and are seeking a different way to organise their work, some because they are politically or socially committed to the ideals of co-operation, some because they are unemployed and have few other alternatives. There are probably a thousand reasons for different co-operators getting together.

In each case, the organisation of the co-operative will reflect the backgrounds of the co-operators and their experience. It might well happen therefore that co-ops in the same trade doing the same things will be organised in completely different ways. Thus one group of co-operators are convinced that a manager with substantial powers is essential to the running of their firm whereas others adopt a more collective approach. Beware of people from outside your co-op who insist that you must have a particular structure. It might not work in your case and might lead to the demise of the co-op. On the other hand, you may find that someone from outside the firm can see things much more clearly and can give you sound advice.

Co-ops that have been set up by a group of professionals or by a local authority are particularly at risk. The outside bodies might insist that good management means having a good manager. This is not necessarily the case. It is important to remember that management is a process not a person and is based on good decision making. Good decision making can be carried out by a co-operative team with a variety of skills and experience better than by one individual manager.

New co-operators who have been working for perhaps half a lifetime on the shopfloor of a traditional firm may take a different view. It is entirely acceptable for those co-operators who wish to exercise their right to participate in management only at the formal meetings of the co-op to do so. It should be remembered that the prospect of participating in decision making without training or experience can be quite frightening especially if the decisions involve substantial sums of money.

Product or service

The particular product or service made or provided by the co-operative firm will substantially affect the type of decision making structure the co-op operates. In some co-ops, the level of skills required for each job is very similar. These co-ops are either in highly skilled areas such as computers or unskilled trades such as cleaners. In these co-ops, there is a mutual understanding of each other's work problems and an inbuilt respect for each person's ability to contribute towards the decision making process.

Where skill levels are highly differentiated within the same co-op, democratic decision making becomes more of a problem. It may therefore be essential to devote more time to the preparation of information for co-op members so that options can be presented clearly and understandably. Otherwise there is a possibility of partially disenfranchising the unskilled co-op members who may not be able to grasp the technical details of some decisions.

In other firms, the decision making process is not critical in terms of time. The decisions that have to be made do not happen on a daily basis but can be saved up till the next meeting of the co-operative. An example would be a small retail shop where there are a number of routine tasks to do during the week but no decisions have to be taken. Decisions about different stock, new lines or shop organisation can be left to the co-operative meeting.

In a manufacturing co-op, and particularly one that does jobbing work, new orders have to be taken, production schedules have to be worked out, supplies ordered, prices quoted, and priorities decided, all on a daily basis.

It is obvious that collective decision making on every issue at a weekly meeting would not work in such a case. Particular decision making responsibilities must be delegated to smaller groups or individuals. It is necessary to work much harder at democratic decision making systems in groups such as these because of the danger of misuse of devolved power.

Size of co-op

The size of a co-operative has a significant bearing on the type of decision making structure that needs to be established. Co-ops vary in size from two person businesses to very large manufacturing firms. At all points on the spectrum there are different problems to overcome in the dual aims of being commercially efficient and democratically sound. When there are only a few members in the co-op, the temptation is to not have any formal decision making structure because you can make decisions as you go along while you are working. This may work very well for the production side of the business but may prove absolutely disastrous in other areas such as finance. However small a co-op, it has a legal responsibility to hold meetings to transact the co-op's business and to record the decisions made. If decisions are not recorded, they get forgotten or misrepresented at subsequent discussions.

As the size of the co-operative grows, it becomes eminently sensible to formalise management and for all members to be involved in meetings. When it becomes impractical and unmanageable for all members to turn up to meetings, an elected delegate structure has to be instituted. Delegates should be elected by all the members or by each department where appropriate. The management committee then runs the business on a mandate established every year.

In very large co-operatives, a controlling board is elected but there is also an appointed management team whose responsibility it is to fulfil the wishes of the co-op and in particular the co-op board, but who themselves might not be members of the co-operative.

A simple guideline on size might be:

2 to 4 members   temptation to make the decision making too informal

5 to 15 members   all members involved in decision making body

15 to 50 members   delegates elected to decision making body

50 plus   delegates elected to decision making body plus executive management staff (who may or may not be members of the co-op)

This is a guideline only and in each co-op a different method will work. It also simply concentrates on how formal decisions take place and does not imply that there are no other management roles in the co-operative. For instance even in a two or three person co-op, there might well be someone who acts as a co-ordinator or manager because it is necessary to have someone who can make instant decisions.

Where do decisions get taken?

What decisions get taken at what meeting is very important to the effectiveness of the co-operative both as a co-op and as a business. Normally co-operatives have three types of meetings: weekly or fortnightly meetings on production-related issues; quarterly meetings on business and policy issues; and general meetings which are usually held just once a year (AGMs). It is worth drawing up ground rules in the co-op about what sorts of issues get discussed at which meetings. For instance:

Production meetings (weekly or fortnightly)
These meetings might discuss production scheduling; ordering; work review; taking on new staff; urgent financial business; reports from officers; correspondence; minor employment matters etc.

Co-operative business meetings (monthly or quarterly)
These meetings are likely to be the formal management meetings of the co-op which have been laid down in the model rules or articles of association. For this reason they need to be well run and detailed minutes need to be kept. Items for discussion might include: finances—including financial reports such as profit and loss accounts; balance sheets and cash flow; membership applications; business planning; wages and conditions; new projects; ideas; purchases; pay and price increases etc.

Annual general meetings
These are also statutory meetings which provide two opportunities: in a larger co-operative, the opportunity for all the members to be involved and in particular to elect the management committee for the coming year (in a very large co-op these meetings could be held quarterly to allow greater

participation); and in all co-ops, the opportunity for members to review the past year and think about the future.

These meetings constitute the formal co-operative decision making processes that must be used to confirm or initiate any programme of action. However, the type of co-op will determine the speed and range of decision making that is required. Where decisions have to be made on a day to day or sometimes an hour to hour basis, the co-operative must have some sort of structure outside its formal meetings. This is likely to involve a manager or a co-ordinator (the words can be used interchangeably because although they imply control from a different direction, the functions are the same).

The idea of meetings and more meetings is anathema to many people. It conjures up a picture of needless bureaucracy, time wasted discussing minutiae and 'committee decisions' which are in reality poor compromises. This is often true. However, meetings are essential to any group structure and if worked at and willingly participated in, they can be effective and even enjoyable. Great importance should be attached to the presentation of information and the chairing of meetings to prevent them falling into any of the traps mentioned above.

Role of the manager/co-ordinator

In many co-operatives (some would say all co-operatives), there is a need to delegate authority to an individual or to a small group of individuals within the co-operative. This must be seen as a delegation of authority by the prime authority which is the general meeting or management committee of the co-op. Attempts to create a management structure with an emphasis on managers controlling the workforce should be resisted. It is frequently co-operative practice to name the individuals to whom authority is delegated co-ordinators rather than managers in order to reinforce this view.

The functions of a manager/co-ordinator within a co-op are:

- making sure that decisions taken at the co-op's meetings are carried out
- reporting back to the co-op on recent performance
- taking decisions independently within an agreed policy framework
- ensuring the commercial success of the co-op

It is important that the manager/co-ordinator should fulfil these functions within the guidelines set by the co-operative and at all times be accountable to the co-operative as a whole. Clear relationships should be established between the co-op and the manager/co-ordinator. Who, for instance, is responsible for which areas and what decisions have to be referred to whom? In some co-ops such as Mondragon, the managers/co-ordinators are not members and do not have a vote at the management meeting of the co-operative.

It is an important principle to remember in co-operatives that managers do not equal management. Management is a process that the members of the co-operative are part of; managers are a means of fulfilling the tasks set by that process. It is certainly worthwhile outlining what decisions managers do not have control over. These must include decisions on staff, particularly decisions to hire and fire, which should always be made by the co-op committee. Capital purchases and general decisions on expansion plans should also not be left to managers/co-ordinators.

One of the functions of managers/co-ordinators is quite clearly to fulfil the co-operative's demands for commercial success. As the co-op grows larger, it might consider the possibility of appointing someone to ensure the success of the enterprise as a co-operative as well. Scott Bader, for instance, has had the services of a commonwealth secretary for a number of years. The job could be considered as a sort of shop steward acting for the co-operative as a whole with the aim of constantly appraising the success of the co-op in reaching its co-operative goals. This role could in fact be seen as an extension of the role of an existing trade union shop steward in collective bargaining. It will be interesting to see developments in this area made by new co-ops over the next few years.

Caucusing

In co-operatives where the decision making processes are inefficient or where the co-op is not prepared to consider putting responsibility into the hands of any one individual or group of individuals, then caucusing may take place. Some individuals within the co-op might end up making decisions through informal discussion because the situation is urgent. This informal but powerful process of decision making is not very co-operative but it has to be recognised and sometimes it has also to be recognised as an efficient system. This does not mean it should be condoned or encouraged. In fact in a proper co-operative, caucusing should be controlled either by formally delegating powers or by recalling them to the co-op meeting.

Leadership

A group of co-operators is not a homogenous mass of people all taking equal part in and responsibility for decision making. Many co-op members may see working in a co-op as merely another job and not wish to take on any other responsibilities in addition to their productive work. Often co-ops, like many other organisations, revolve around a few key people who are the driving force behind the firm and take the others along with them. The principle of 'from each according to ability and to each according to need' is a rich underlying vein in co-operative thought.

Leadership is therefore not an issue which should be ignored. The organisation of a co-op must be sufficiently flexible to allow for the personal ambitions of such members as long as they can be held in check when necessary. It may be equally important to ensure that not all the 'leaders' are part of the management/co-ordination team but that they are balanced by strong views from the shop floor. There is certainly a case for all managers/co-ordinators to be transferred to shop floor jobs on a regular basis to ensure a balance between workforce and co-ordinators. There is also a strong case for all manager/co-ordinator roles to be filled by internal appointments.

Running Meetings

Effective decision making on important issues in co-operatives happens at meetings of co-operative members. Meetings must therefore be efficiently and productively run. Without good decision making at meetings, the co-operative's social and business efficiency drops and decisions begin to be made outside meetings, effectively removing some members from the decision making process. On such an informal level those who like each other or know each other best become a sort of central core which those who have less in common cannot participate in.

Meetings formalise discussion and should, if handled well, decrease the authority of the knowledgeable and increase the participation of the timid.

Agendas

Agendas of meetings should be prepared in advance either by the officers (chair, secretary or treasurer) or by leaving a notice on the noticeboard where all members (even those not on management committees) can put up items for discussion. This gives members the chance to think about the issue before the meeting. Items placed on the agenda must be relevant to the type of meeting it is. There is no point in putting a discussion of the co-op's constitution on the agenda of a weekly meeting: this is the sort of thing that gets discussed at a monthly or special meeting. Papers about any items on the agenda which require some digesting, such as financial information, should be circulated in advance of the meeting wherever possible (see **Financial information for co-op members**)

Timing

There are a variety of views on when is the best time to hold co-operative meetings. A logical time might seem to be either Friday afternoon or Monday morning for weekly meetings in order to have a review of the past week and look forward to the coming week. However there can be disadvantages. On Fridays, people may want to get away. On Monday mornings, you may discover the Monday morning feeling. Many co-ops hold their meetings on a midweek morning or afternoon, sometimes in the evening. Some co-ops hold their meetings in the members' time, others in work time. The former does have the advantage that you do not lose productive time, but the benefits of recognising that meetings and thus the management of the co-operative are 'work' functions is not to be underestimated.

Attendance

Turning up on time to meetings should be seen by members as a duty to each other and to the co-operative. There is nothing more frustrating than sitting around waiting for others to finish a piece of work or arrive in the morning. If meetings are held in work time, the co-operative also suffers because productive time is wasted. In fact holding meetings in work time may be a good way to encourage attendance.

If a co-op member stops turning up to meetings or only appears intermittently, the co-op as a whole suffers—it becomes less democratic and less worker controlled. If the problem becomes very serious, a co-operative could choose to exercise sanctions against the member. Again if meetings are held in work time, the problem is lessened as the member who does not attend does not get paid for that time. It is essential that decision making and management should be seen as part of the job description of co-op members.

Chairing

Co-op meetings should have a chairperson. The purpose is to help members stick to the agenda, introduce items and put together an analysis of the decisions arrived at. Being a chairperson is a skilful job and also a powerful one. Some co-ops choose to have a permanent chair elected annually to recognise the skill; some rotate the chair each meeting to recognise the power and contain it. It is an important skill to gain because it gives people a real insight into the way meetings decide and improves on the contribution that those individuals can make to subsequent meetings. It must be recognised however that some people have more aptitude for it than others. It might well be worthwhile, in an important meeting, choosing a skilled chairperson so that important decisions are reached effectively.

Minute taking

Like chairing, minute taking may also be rotated or carried out by one person. It is a very important role because if decisions are not recorded or not recorded properly, they will get forgotten or be misrepresented. It is not necessary to record every single sentence, comment or opinion but notes of the substance of the discussion, divergent opinions and most importantly decisions made and who should follow them up. Votes should also be recorded as well as any major information items such as monthly financial reports. Notes should be legible or typed and should be put into the co-operative's minute book. The formal responsibility for keeping minutes rests with the elected secretary of the co-op but the actual task can be delegated to others with the secretary ensuring that it is carried out.

The minute book can be used as the bible of the co-operative. It records all the decisions of the co-operative, all the secondary rules and usually the primary ones as well, staff taken on and those sacked, members accepted and rejected, the names and addresses of the members and their shareholdings etc. Looking back through past records of a co-operative can be very illuminating.

Voting/consensus/abstentions

When there are divergent opinions within the decision making body or management committee, how are these resolved? In all cases there should be an appropriate amount of discussion and provision of information—appropriate, that is, to the importance of the topic. It is important to decide on the issues that require a quick decision, those that require detailed information on the options to be prepared, those decisions which will take some time to come to, and those that shouldn't be taken at the meeting at all. One method of getting through the agenda is to set a timetable for each item—five minutes on production targets, two hours on pay awards etc. This obviously depends on having a good chair and the timing may have to be revised as you go along because some issues have wider implications than originally anticipated.

When sufficient time has been left for discussion of the topic, how is the decision made? Many co-ops make decisions by trying to move towards a consensus on particular items. This in effect means discussing items until there is a generally held view that there is only one alternative. Pride is often taken in the fact that the meetings never have to take votes. It can be effective for many decisions, but the following points should be borne in mind. Firstly, the process is time consuming which militates against efficient decision making but it does also allow for full discussion and full participation from members. It can on the other hand stifle contributions from quieter members and can be used by stronger members as a means of steamrollering a decision through which is much resented later on. It does not of course give the opportunity to members to record a vote against the decision (which would be important for those members if things go wrong with the decision).

Generally speaking, there is nothing wrong with voting. It is relatively normal that in any decision there is a majority and a minority, although within co-operatives one hopes there would be a large measure of agreement. It is however important that members accept decisions that go against them. If the same issue keeps returning for discussion, it can create bad feeling within the co-op. Votes, of course, should be recorded in the minute book.

Abstentions may be necessary when members genuinely cannot decide or in situations where they have a particular personal interest in the outcome. If they are a frequent occurrence, however, they can be very destructive. It usually means that there has not been enough discussion of the issue or that the positive advantages of the decision are not apparent enough to the abstainees. It is also very awkward when members are unable to make difficult decisions and will abstain rather than commit themselves. A classic case of this would concern decisions on sacking of employees or members where there is obviously a lot of personal involvement. It is incumbent on members however to make decisions in these instances rather than wash their hands of it and conveniently blame those that are prepared to make the decision. The largest number of abstentions we have come across in a co-op was five out of a total of thirteen members on a major policy issue. The proposers had six votes and there were two votes against. Less than half the members therefore were in favour of the proposal. Although in theory it had been approved, needless to say the proposal was not carried out.

Responsibilities of officers

The constitution of a co-operative usually provides for the election of a number of officers. The functions of these officers are to look after the interests of the co-operative as a separate legal entity and to act as a formal link both internally with its members and also with the outside world.

The officers usually include:

the secretary who is responsible for (which does not necessarily mean that she or he does the work) the running of the co-operative as a whole. This would include keeping the minutes of members' meetings; keeping the co-operative's seal; noting changes to the constitution and the addition of secondary rules; keeping a record of members; issuing share certificates; and keeping records of members' shares or loans.

the treasurer who is responsible for the financial side of the co-op, which includes keeping regular books of account, preparing annual accounts with the auditors and presenting financial information to other co-operative members. Again the treasurer may not be the one who does the work but she or he has to ensure that it is done.

Sometimes co-operatives choose to have joint secretaries and treasurers as a method of training other members in order to ensure continuity if staff leave.

Some co-op constitutions also have a standing chairperson (sic) who is annually elected. This is actually rare as their role is usually restricted to running meetings and representing the co-op to the outside world. Co-ops usually rotate their chair at meetings, but this is not a requirement.

Internal relations

There are a number of different issues that need to be tackled by the co-operative concerning the way it organises itself internally and the way members of the group relate to each other both as people and as employees. These will not be resolved at the beginning of the co-op's life but will develop as an organic structure which is added to as the nature of the co-operative changes through growth or turnover of personnel. Apart from the issues examined below, trade union membership is an extremely important aspect of internal relations in a co-op and it is fully discussed later in the section on **Employment in a co-op**.

Taking on new employees

Co-operatives must have a policy of open membership to fit in with the definition established by the International Co-operative Alliance. However in the case of workers co-operatives, this is only relevant when there is a vacancy caused by expansion or by a member leaving. Members will be added only sporadically and, as mentioned earlier in the handbook, will only become members after a probationary period. Thus in workers co-ops 'open membership' means that the co-operative does not discriminate against potential members on the grounds of race, politics, religion or sex. It does however raise the issue of how new employees who are likely to become members are taken on. Each co-operative will approach recruitment policy differently but decisions will have to be reached about such things as:

- what is the relative importance given to production skills and commitment to co-operative principles and practice in the choice between new employees?
- will you state in the advert that you are a co-operative or will you just ask for specific skills?
- will you ask on the application form or in the interview a range of questions about applicants' attitudes to co-operatives?
- will you all interview the candidates or appoint somebody or a group to choose, or at least do some sifting of applicants?
- are members conscious that it is perhaps one of their most important tasks to get the right new workers? The co-operative is interviewing not just for a new worker but also for a manager and owner at the same time.
- will you be adopting a positive action policy in your employment practices towards, for example, women, ethnic minorities and young people?

- if you are having difficulty filling a post, are you willing to offer higher wages and/or better conditions or will this skew the co-operative's internal organisation?
- do you want the new job holder to be a member of the co-operative?
- will you offer the new employee a permanent position or a short-term contract until the probationary period is up?
- do you require new employees to become members if their probationary period is satisfactory?

Turnover of staff

One interesting development in many new co-operatives is the high turnover of staff. In some cases this produces a completely new group of people from the founder members within a relatively short period of time. Ironically, this is in complete contrast to many of the established producer co-operatives on the continent which have problems with many of the older members not leaving. There are three possible explanations for the turnover of staff in new co-ops in Britain: firstly, the common pattern among younger people nowadays of moving jobs after two or three years; secondly, the amount of hard work and effort at the beginning of the co-operative burning out the founder members; and thirdly, because co-ops tend to be relatively conservative institutions, they sometimes fail to give individuals the opportunity to pursue personal aims and ambitions which the co-operative is unwilling to incorporate. This can lead to key members leaving (in particular those who are fulfilling management functions) which is detrimental to the co-operative. Lending institutions might also be wary of high staff turnover as a long-term loan might well end up being repaid by a completely different set of people from the original borrowers. There could also be a loss of commitment to the ideals in a particular co-op if there are too many new members, although new ideals may replace the old.

One advantage of staff turnover is that it reaffirms the principles of common ownership and co-operation. No individual member owns her or his job but only controls it whilst she or he is employed. Members pass jobs on when they leave and do not take the capital and the firm with them. Some co-operatives say they do not want to take on loans and other responsibilities because if they stop trading, they can go their own way. This is a denial of the nature of co-operative jobs which should be jobs retained for the future as well as the present.New members also bring new energies and enthusiasm to the co-op and as long as they are not weighed down too much by the existing members and their 'way of doing things', this can be very important in taking the co-op on to new strengths.

Obviously not all co-operatives have a high turnover of staff and it is significant that those that are either more ambitious or have higher wage levels or have been going longer tend to be much more stable in their membership. It is quite often a mixture of some of the founders and most of the members taken on in the first two years that provides the basic driving force for the co-operative.

Wages

The majority of modern co-operatives operate a system of equal wages throughout the co-operative whatever skills are required for different jobs, as mentioned earlier in **Rules and secondary rules**. It is important that co-ops think about the implications of this practice particularly as co-ops have to operate within a market economy. Firstly, co-op members whose wages in other firms or organisations would normally be lower than their co-op wages are less likely to leave the co-op. This can be a positive reason for adopting an equal pay structure, although some would say that it is more difficult to 'get rid of' these workers if they are not doing a good job because they have more incentive to stay. A more difficult problem is that those posts within the co-operative which command higher wages in the rest of the economy (eg management posts) may be difficult to fill and when filled it may be difficult to keep the employee. Co-operatives usually get round this problem by making internal appointments to these posts from the existing workforce or by appointing people at higher wages but not allowing them membership of the co-operative. Internal appointments are probably better as this ensures continuity and also provides opportunities for people to realise personal ambitions within the co-operative. Equal wages are not essential to the co-operative principle although if there are inequalities, differentials should be depressed. Certainly in a larger enterprise, equal wages would be virtually impossible.

Member investment

ICOM model rules do not require members to put capital into their co-operative (apart from the £1 nominal share). This seems to be the right basis to work from as workers do not necessarily have access to lump sums for investment.

However because of the difficulties of raising finance without individual investment, members often have to put up some money either as a lump sum, a deduction from wages or personal guarantees on loans or overdrafts. Although unsatisfactory, the investment of members' money is almost inevitable as most lending institutions see the co-operators' money as the primary risk money. This raises questions of which members commit money and how much. It is sensible in our view to ensure as much equality of investment between co-operators as possible. For instance, every member could put in £500 or £1,000. If loans made by different members are very unequal or some members don't put any money in, those who have made big loans feel the co-op is more important to them than the others. If differentials exist, it is sensible to reduce them as much as possible by repaying larger loans out of profits or by increasing investments from other members by regular amounts.

Personal relationships

In a small co-operative the composition of the membership and the members' individual personalities are a significant factor in the running of the co-operative and its ultimate success both as a business and a co-operative. How those individuals are able to work together and how antagonisms are resolved must be seen as important to the survival of the co-op. Worker co-operatives are not communes. Co-ops are associations of people in their working lives. Co-operators share common cause only in the thirty-five to forty hours of the working week. Members are not required to share any other part of their lives unlike communes where people live together, eat together and work together.

This restriction of co-operation to the purely economic front can create its own difficulties and distortions. When co-operators come from widely different financial circumstances, attitudes to work and success vary enormously. Those who have personal financial resources outside the co-operative could consider the co-operative as an interesting temporary diversion rather than a means of supporting themselves into the future. This may well have an effect on the sort of structures that are built up within the co-operative and on the financial performance of the co-op. Similarly, the demands of others for a better life style in financial terms might well conflict with those who wish to explore different ways of working which take account of people's psychological and emotional needs.

In a small group, personal antagonisms need to be resolved. Worker co-operation is a very intense experience and if personal battles cannot be resolved, consideration must be given to one of the members leaving the co-operative. At the opposite extreme there are dangers in getting too emotionally involved with other members of the co-operative as this slightly distorts the democratic framework of the co-op. It is best to avoid becoming sexually or emotionally involved with other co-op members if possible. Other distortions can occur when many members from the same family work in the group. If there are too many, questions can be raised about the nature of the co-op as a true co-op. If over fifty per cent of the members are from the same family, it is a matter of debate whether it is a co-op even though it is formally registered with co-op rules.

Minority interests must also be protected within a co-operative. The very nature of democratic decision making means there is usually a minority against any proposal. This is not normally a problem as most members learn to accept it if decisions go against them. However if a group of members are consistently in the minority when decisions about the direction of the co-op are taken, thought must be given to the fact that there are effectively two co-ops operating rather than one. For effective operation, similarity of direction is essential. One possibility might be to reach a compromise which takes account of the demands of the minority. The ultimate solution would be to spin off a new co-op to enable the dissenting group to set up a different, more satisfactory structure.

Outside membership

One of the questions that has exercised many of those involved in the co-operative movement is whether to exclude or include members who do not actually work within the enterprise. Essentially in a *workers* co-operative, outside membership is not acceptable. However, many argue that outsiders should be included on the grounds that extra support, advice, involvement and sometimes capital are needed.

Non-worker members are created in two ways. Firstly, they may be founder members of the co-operative who, unless they resign or are removed by one other method, have a right to remain in membership in perpetuity. Quite often co-operatives have less than seven members when they start which means they either register under the Companies Act which requires only two members or they have 'sleeping' or non-working members. Under ICOM model rules, non-working founder members may be removed when a co-operative with at least seven employed members applies to the Registrar of Friendly Societies for a 'certificate of common ownership'.

The second way that outside members may be created is when co-ops feel the need to get advice and support from people outside who have special skills or experience. Some co-operatives (such as newspapers) want to involve their customers or the community in their organisation. These are understandable motives but the ownership and control structure must be clear from the outset. In particular, the rights of employees in any given situation must be unambiguous. Trade unions are very important here. A support or friends' group might be an alternative option to outside membership in such cases.

Other 'co-ops' with very peculiar rules take outside members who provide capital. This can be distorting and sometimes destructive. A Bristol printers co-op, for instance, was closed down by outside shareholders cashing in on increased share values and many workers lost their jobs.

Co-ops which are set up by non-workers on behalf of workers are usually subject to outside members because the founders want to keep control. In these cases it is difficult to create a genuine co-operative enterprise and it might be better to set up a community business or municipal enterprise instead.

In general outside members do not rely on the co-operative for their livelihood. It is not critical to them if they make a decision which has a damaging effect on the co-operative. For this reason, their power and responsibility should be limited. Outside membership of non-workers is contrary to the practice of workers' control in co-operatives, although in some cases there are practical and political advantages in such membership. These advantages should not however be used to dilute the principle of workers control.

Future rewards

It is important that those who set up a co-operative and go through the almost inevitable period of sacrifice in so doing (both in terms of hard work and low wages), should have the possibility of some future reward. This is not only important for them as individuals but for the proper development of the co-operative. It is not unknown for members coming in when the co-operative is more firmly established to be resented by the original members. If there is a mechanism for the original members to be rewarded for their work in setting up the co-operative, feelings of resentment will not be translated into attempts to retain control of the co-operative.

Mechanisms might include:
- extra hours that are put in at the beginning may be recorded as a loan to the co-operative and repaid when it is profitable
- donations, gifts and ex gratia payments may be made to the founders of the co-operative for their special services to the co-operative
- loans with or without interest may be made to new co-operatives formed by outgoing members. This is particularly important for members wanting to start up in another area but who do not wish to start from scratch again.

Such mechanisms should not necessarily always be applied. The start up period of a new co-operative is often the most enjoyable time (if poorly paid) and doing a nine to five job later on (even if better paid) may not be so great. The original founders may also have been novices at the start and not been as productive as they now are. Indeed, they may well have made some bad investment decisions which the current members are still paying for.

Financial information for co-op members

All the decisions, programmes and plans of any business must be costed and assessed for their financial soundness. Similarly the results of any plan and of general trading must be recorded and analysed. Co-operatives are no exception to this. Indeed fuller information is needed in a co-operative because everyone is involved in decision making. Firstly, there is a legal obligation on the members to run the business in a proper fashion if the protection of limited liability is not to be forfeited. Secondly, the co-operative cannot be run on a truly democratic basis if knowledge and information about the two most important aspects of the business are in the hands of only one or two people.

People often say 'I don't know anything about money or accounts.' In fact, if someone can deal with their own financial affairs, then they can deal with the co-operative's finances. There are three ways of facilitating this:

- as many members as possible should be involved directly in book-keeping, costing jobs, and the preparation of budgets and cashflows
- relevant financial information should be presented regularly to the members in a form that can be readily understood by everybody
- if necessary, time and resources have to be earmarked for training in this field.

The type of information that should be included in a monthly financial report is as follows:

Receipts and payments
what money has been received and spent in the month and how this compares with the cash flow forecast

Current position
a comparison of the current assets and liabilities to show the true position of the business

Break-even analysis
an analysis of the months's actual production and/or trading against costs to check that it is not being run at a loss.

At general meetings of the co-operative, more detailed financial information should be prepared for co-op members including:

Accounts

These should include a balance sheet and a profit and loss account and should be audited by an accountant. The problem with these accounts is that they tend to be well out of date, sometimes appearing six months to a year after the end of a financial year. This means they are not very useful as a planning tool. Less detailed, and therefore less accurate, management accounts appearing soon after the relevant period has ended are the most useful tool in co-operative decision making.

Market analysis

A detailed analysis of customers where relevant should usually be submitted to a general meeting. Obviously this is impossible with a retail business but in other businesses an analysis can be made of the success in various types of market, what volume for each of those markets was achieved against predicted sales etc. From this information a customer profile can be built up to determine the potential level of subsidy possible for the coming year. A percentage analysis of regular customers against one-offs can also be made.

Creditors and debtors should also be examined to discover any particular problems with persistent bad debtors. Decisions can then be taken on credit-worthiness.

Budget for the coming year

This is the other main area where members must be fully involved in the running of the business. The budget might include such things as the level of wages for the coming year, productivity targets for wage increases, planned profit levels, determination of profit distribution, cost reductions, new expansion or staffing plans etc.

For the enterprise to be able to function properly as a co-operative, it is essential that the costs involved in setting up and operating the structure the members want are budgeted for as an integral part of central budget planning. Desirable programmes such as in-service training as part of a system of job rotation should not be approached in budgetting terms as purely a cost burden. It is fairly easy to quantify the cost but less easy to measure the benefits which should be considerable both in terms of the flexibility of the workforce and individual job satisfaction.

Unless these items are properly costed and budgetted for, there will always be a tendency for them to be regarded as peripheral rather than as part of the structure of the business. They will always be the first things to go if costs have to be cut. If not budgetted for but still operated, they will add hidden costs to the business. Doing a proper budgetting exercise means that what the members regard as the most important aspects of the internal structure can be sorted out since it is unlikely that everything that is thought to be desirable can be afforded, particularly in the early stages of a co-operative. Further improvements can then be introduced as the business becomes more established. This approach should help to prevent the members becoming disillusioned with the co-operative structure if things don't go as expected.

The four areas of costs to be considered when drawing up a budget are:

- **structure of democratic management**

Whatever the co-operative decides about the number and form of meetings it requires, it is vital that attendance at these meetings is treated as part of the work of the members and not something extra, unpaid and voluntary. Therefore attendance at meetings and participation in management should be part of the contract of employment and paid, even if the cost has to be evened out across the hourly rate. Provision of facilities for members with children to attend meetings should also be a priority. These costs should be treated as part of the administration budget.

- **training**

The provision of training, both in-service and external, is one of the most productive investments a co-operative can make. The long-term benefit is a more skilled, flexible and productive workforce but initial costs can be high and must be budgetted for. This means not only the readily identifiable costs of courses run in the workplace and outside in terms of training materials, tutor hours and loss of working time, but also the costs in loss of productivity in handing over jobs from one member to another in a system of job rotation. Even if there is a probationary period for new employees, it is essential that they feel part of the co-operative from the beginning so provision for an induction course should be considered.

- **pay and conditions**

No aspect of pay and conditions should be ignored in budgets. This means not only major items like pay increases but also provision of child care facilities, full sick pay, improved maternity pay down to the cost of a day spent discussing the co-operative's affairs. One of the potentially most damaging situations in a co-operative is if the members are faced with cutting their wages or cutting back on their conditions of employment. It should not be forgotten that the members of a co-operative are employees with all the legal rights this implies and wildly fluctuating conditions of employment are not acceptable. Proper costing of changes in working conditions can help avoid problems of this sort. So all proposals to change pay and working conditions should be accompanied by costings. The other side of this coin is that there should be some independent forum in the co-operative to consider aspects of pay and conditions outside the pressure of a management meeting, ie a trade union meeting where members can consider their wages and conditions from a different point of view.

- **social and charitable aims**

Most co-operatives have aims beyond just providing jobs for their members. These can be political aims, aims associated with their particular industry, a wish to be of service in the local community or other charitable aims. The costs involved here can be dealt with either as part of the central budget so money can be allocated during the year or as part of the distribution of profits. Clearly having a specific budget means that money is more likely to be spent in this area. Hidden costs, such as offering lower prices to some customers or free use of facilities, should not be forgotten.

Community involvement

Co-ops are not just isolated, independent, self-concerned organisations—or at least they shouldn't be. Most co-ops exist in communities that the members wish to serve in various ways. If co-op members do not have these wider aims and ambitions, the co-op loses much of its driving force and becomes merely a mutual aid society where workers are only interested in gaining further reward for themselves.

The communities which co-ops serve might be geographical areas, but they might also be particular sections of the community such as campaigning groups, charities etc. Or co-ops might reject one or more different types of customer whom they find unacceptable for social or political reasons. Thus co-ops might reject racist or sexist work or might reject customers in particular trades such as the arms trade. This negative response is much easier to trigger in some types of activity than in others. For example it is more difficult to determine the attitudes of one's customers in a retail shop than it is if one is a printer.

Better products

One of the original Rochdale pioneer principles was 'to supply pure and unadulterated produce'. This was because the quality of much of the food and produce sold at that time was so variable. Striving for better quality and care in the making of products has always been a part of socialist and co-operative planning. The problem of bad food and produce is not of course as great in the 1980s as it was in the nineteenth century because of the introduction of trading standards and many other legal provisions and powers. However the majority of co-operatives are still very concerned about quality. The enormous number of co-operatives in the wholefood sector demonstrates the concern co-operators have for the quality of their product. In fact existing wholefood co-op shops have very similar origins to the original consumer co-op societies of the nineteenth century. In France and Italy, many contracts have been awarded to co-operative firms because their work was better than that of capitalist enterprises.

The desire of co-operatives to produce better products may have unwanted results. Firstly by insisting on quality the costs of production soar and the co-op ends up having to sell its goods to richer sections of the community.

Concomitant with the desire to produce quality products is the desire to make these products available to a wide range of people. To achieve this and survive commercially co-operators might well have to make sacrifices either by working longer hours, paying themselves less money or being ultra-efficient. Notwithstanding these difficulties, a fundamental premise for the new co-operative movement is 'production for need rather than profit'. In practice, the two have to be balanced to ensure survival.

Subsidies

A co-operative can decide that some customers should be offered preferential rates or service. For instance prices of goods could be varied according to which customer was buying. If it was a charity or an unwaged individual, they could be offered a cheaper price. If the company was a large company or part of government, a higher price could be charged. The end result is that profitable concerns subsidise those in a less fortunate position. The co-operative can act as a redistributor of wealth on a small scale. One must of course assess the costs of producing and selling the goods but margins can be determined at a level in between the two price levels. As long as the customer mix is right, there should be no problem. It is important to understand the financial process you are involved in when giving subsidies or preferential rates. In budgetting, the co-op must set its hourly rates or unit costs so that it is able to make its required profit level as well as underwrite its subsidy to customers. It is no good charging labour at £5 an hour to ninety-five per cent of your customers if that means you are losing £1 an hour for each hour that you are paid. What a co-op is doing by giving a subsidy is distributing part of its profits in advance to customers. Again a balance must be struck here between the need for future investment or indeed survival and the need to fulfil social and political aims. It may be better to distribute your profits after you have made them rather than as you go along if you are unsure about the financial processes involved.

Co-op intertrading and federating

An ambition of co-operators for the past 100 years has been the creation of a 'co-operative commonwealth'. The concept of an economy built on interlinked co-operatives all independently run but sharing a common aim is perhaps a pipe dream which could never be converted into reality. The dream seems further away in 1984 than it has ever been. However this does not diminish the important premise that co-ops linked together can form a far stronger force than the sum of their parts. The co-op retail movement, for instance, although in decline now, has gained enormous strength by linking together. Co-operation between co-operatives was also one of the important principles laid down by the Rochdale pioneers in the last century.

To ensure the survival of worker co-operatives in the latter part of the twentieth century, co-ops must direct as much of their trade as possible towards other co-ops. In this way co-ops can form a strong base from which to grow stronger both economically and socially. The Mondragon system in northern Spain is a fine example of this sort of co-operation and interlinking of enterprises. Links should be forged between co-ops in the same geographical area as well as those in the same trades. Federated structures should also be built up to ensure close communication and the possibility of joint policy and decision making.

Outside advice/insularity/secondary co-ops

There tends to be a great deal of antagonism among co-ops to pressure or advice from people or organisations outside co-operatives. Co-op members are determined to preserve the hard won privilege of controlling their economic lives and ways of working. This is correct. Outside agencies and individuals should not try to take control of the co-op's decisions as this directly contradicts the co-op's raison d'être. Thus 'godfathers' (or outside advisers) on the Mondragon model are rejected by co-ops who see them as an intrusion rather than an aid to survival.

This assertive independence may however breed an insularity and a mistrust of the outside world which can prove detrimental to the co-op's success. Co-ops have to operate in the real world which means a market economy which actively discourages the setting up of systems whereby labour controls capital rather than the other way round. Many local authorities are now trying to encourage co-ops and co-ops must learn to work with them in order to oppose other pressures.

One half-way house between insularity and independence which is also important for the growth of the co-op movement is the development of secondary co-operatives. These are most likely to succeed on either a sector level, for example in building, or by geographical areas. It is important that co-operatives learn to co-operate with each other—this is one of the fundamental co-operative rules.

Social audits

The continuing pressure on co-ops for economic survival can have an effect on the running of the firm in co-operative terms. If the survival of the firm depends on a strong management team or workers having to make sacrifices on the way, then it can sometimes be difficult to re-establish the means by which the whole workforce can be involved in decision making and gain the benefits of co-operation which are not merely financial. Indeed the inertia created by the system that produced the successful firm might mean there was no incentive to demand restructuring.

However, co-operation is about a process not a product, about people and relationships rather than mechanical answers and static environments. Co-operatives should always be re-evaluating themselves to assess the potential of new ways of organising, new ways of dealing with problems, new ways of dealing with success and new ways of dealing with its products, its workforce, its market, and its customers.

Co-ops which have been trading and surviving or succeeding for some time may therefore find it helpful to undertake a social audit. This is in contrast to a normal accountancy audit which only looks at the financial performance of the company over the past year and the value of the co-op at the present time. A social audit is a method of assessing the performance of the co-op as a co-operative rather than as a business.

A social audit would cover the following areas:

- decision making processes and their relative successes and failures with particular regard to the involvement of the whole workforce
- education and training of members and the outside community
- involvement in the local community
- production practices and organisation with regard to improving the quality of jobs
- employment practices and their development
- analysis of markets with a view to determining new directions and the desirability of discriminating for or against particular customers
- determining levels of subsidy for particular customers
- analysis of type of product in terms of social usefulness

Employment in a co-op

The members of a co-operative are both employers and employees. As employers they have a wide range of responsibilities and as employees a wide range of rights under the law. Despite the complexities this can cause, in many ways it puts members of a co-operative in an advantageous position.

Co-operatives are often thought of as bad employers and in particular as offering poor rates of pay and basic conditions of employment. This is largely due to the fact that most new co-operatives are small and under capitalised. Taking a longer view, there is no reason why co-operatives should not be model employers within the financial constraints imposed by their trading position. However, it is important that the members do not assume that because they are a co-operative, their obligations as employers can be ignored. One of the great advantages of co-operatives is that the employees can decide their own wages and conditions according to their individual and collective needs and priorities. This is particularly so in the areas of pay differentials, holidays, childcare provisions and working hours.

It is central to the idea of a workers co-operative that the working members are employed and not self-employed. Self-employed people are by definition pursuing their own individual self-interest and so a 'co-operative' of self-employed people is more like a business partnership or marketing co-operative. The 'co-operative' is no more than an agreement among the individuals involved to market their individual skills. A registered workers co-operative on the other hand, as a limited company, has a legal personality. It can hold assets and be sued in its own name. The people involved do not exercise ownership and control over this organisation as individuals but as employees. Membership is defined in terms of employment and is lost when someone leaves the co-operative.

Membership and employment

Co-operative rules allow reasonable restrictions on the rights of employees to become members of a co-operative. The most common restriction is where new employees are required to undergo a probationary period before being allowed to become members. Some of the implications of probationary periods and other possible restrictions such as limiting membership to employees working over a certain number of hours a week are discussed in the section on **Rules and secondary rules**.

Once somebody becomes a member, they are both employer and employee. Workers undergoing probationary periods, however, are solely employees and have no vote in the running of the co-operative. Their employers are the existing members of the co-op. It is most important that the rights of these people as employees are not forgotten and proper attention is paid to their transfer to membership. In particular, hire and fire and grievance procedures must be properly worked out and the responsibility for carrying them out allocated and known to everyone concerned.

Employment law

There is a mass of legislation which relates either directly or indirectly to employment. However, both in terms of cost and range, the legal obligations of employers to their employees are significantly less than in other advanced industrial countries. The main Acts we shall be concerned with are the Employment Protection (Consolidation) Act 1978 which incorporates previous Employment Protection Acts such as the Contracts of Employment Act 1972; the Redundancy Payments Acts 1965; the Conservative Employment Acts 1980 and 1982 and the various Acts concerning discrimination and health and safety. It should be remembered that new legislation is regularly being introduced so it's worth checking what has happened since the time this was written.

Contracts of employment

There is a lot of confusion over the question of contracts of employment. As soon as someone starts work, a contract exists and is just as valid whether written down or not. It consists of the terms and conditions which the employer offers and the employee accepts in taking on the job. It may be subsequently altered by changes agreed in these terms and conditions not only on an individual basis but also as part of collective bargaining processes. It is also affected by what either party actually does. For example if an employee began to work longer hours or an employer to pay at higher rates on a regular basis, even without formal agreement, this would become part of the contract of employment on the basis of 'custom and practice'. The validity of contracts may also be affected by wider considerations of custom and practice within the industry. A fixed term contract is simply one without periods of notice on either side and which terminates on a set date.

As part of a contract of employment under the common law, there are several general obligations implied but not spelled out on both employers and employees:

Employers:
- to pay wages and salaries for work done
- not to make unauthorised deductions from pay
- to provide work (in some cases)
- to ensure safe working conditions
- to obey the law in general
- to give time off in certain circumstances

Employees:
- to do agreed work
- to obey lawful and reasonable instructions
- to take reasonable care in their work, ie not to cause damage or injury
- not to give away confidential information about the business
- to work only for their employer during agreed working hours. This implies, for example, that written material produced during working hours is the property of the co-operative and not the individual.

Although a contract exists in any employment situation and does not need to be written down, its details are obviously much clearer if they are on paper and any good employer should provide such written details for their employees. (See **Appendix 2 Specimen contract of employment.**)

Written statement of conditions of employment

An employer is required to issue a written statement of the main terms and conditions of employment to each new employee within thirteen weeks of the start of employment. It should be stressed that this statement is not in itself a legal contract but a statement of the main points or information list. The statement should contain the following points:

1 **Name of employer** This should be the registered name of the co-operative.

2 **Name of employee**

3 **Date employment started** This is important for calculating entitlement to all sorts of benefits (see **Appendix 1**). Continuous service from previous employment, such as in a company before it became a co-op, should be included.

4 **Job title** This does not have to be all-embracing. A general description will do. In a co-operative some mention of job rotation and management responsibilities may be appropriate.

5 **Rate of pay** or method or calculating it. This should include all forms of pay such as overtime pay. Again this is most important in calculating a whole range of benefits.

6 **Intervals of pay** When wages are paid, ie weekly or monthly, and whether a week or month in hand.

7 **Hours of work and normal working hours** In a co-operative these should include attendance at management meetings.

8 **Holidays** Annual, public and other holidays and rates of holiday pay should be stated. There is no statutory right to paid holidays except in certain industries covered by wages councils. It is important that even if not detailed in the statement, attention is drawn to the co-operative's secondary rules as to when holidays can be taken, the system for notification, what extra unpaid holidays are allowed and whether holidays can be carried over into the following year.

9 **Sick pay** Provisions over and above the government's statutory sick pay scheme should be outlined.

10 **Pensions** All employees are part of the government scheme, paid for out of national insurance contributions, unless their employer has contracted out into an approved private scheme. It is also possible to have a 'ride-on-top' scheme whereby extra employer and/or employee contributions are made in addition to the state scheme.

11 **Periods of notice** Legal minimum periods of notice are laid down in the Employment Protection (Consolidation) Act 1978. These can be extended but if not the legal minimum must be stated. The minimum periods are:
Less than 4 weeks continuous employment None
4 weeks to 2 years Employer — 1 week. Employee — 1 week.
2 years to 12 years Employer — 1 week for every year of continuous employment. Employee — 1 week.
12 years and more Employer — 12 weeks. Employee — 1 week.
It should be noted that payment in lieu of notice is permissible and that in cases of 'gross misconduct', agreed notice periods may be invalidated.

12 **Disciplinary rules** The 1978 Act requires that employers have a set of rules and procedures to deal with discipline and disputes. This will be dealt with in a subsequent section.

13 **Named person or body** to whom an employee can apply in the event of dissatisfaction with a disciplinary decision or with a grievance.

14 **Grievance procedure**

There are several omissions from the statement, the most glaring of which are maternity and paternity rights. Co-operatives may also want to refer to compassionate leave and training provisions.

It should be noted that under the law an employer can keep a master document to refer an employee to rather than issue individual documents to each employee. Keeping the statement updated can be a problem and changes should be notified within one month of implementation or agreement.

We shall now look in more detail at sick pay, pensions, disciplinary rules and grievance procedure leading up to the thorny question of dismissal.

Sick pay

Sick pay comes in two forms: that paid by the employer and that paid by the state on the basis of national insurance contributions. State sick pay has always been inadequate and is even more so under the statutory sick pay scheme introduced in April 1983. In view of this any good employer should make provision for sick pay over and above the minimum legal requirements. Normally this means topping up state sick pay to full wages for a reasonable period of time. Many employers have a period of full pay followed by a period of half pay.

The statutory sick pay (SSP) scheme is basically a shuffling of the bureaucratic cards which has transferred responsibility for paying and administering the old sickness benefit from the DHSS to employers. It has also made state sick pay taxable. Employees whose average weekly earnings are below the weekly earnings limit for national insurance contributions do not qualify.

In order to qualify for SSP payments, an employee must have been off work sick for four consecutive days, including normal days off. The first three days are 'waiting days' and no SSP is payable. Evidence of sickness is by self-certificate for the first six days; doctor's certificates are now only issued for periods of one week or more. The employer has some latitude in deciding 'qualifying days' for payment (ie the days on which SSP is payable to the employee) but there is no reason why these should not be normal working days. The weekly rate of SSP is set by the government and the maximum payable in any one year or period of sickness is eight weeks. The co-operative, as employer, pays SSP out of its own resources as part of wages and then reclaims it by deduction from the usual PAYE tax and NI contributions forwarded to the Inland Revenue collector of taxes every month.

SSP is clearly inadequate in two particular respects: the level of benefits is low and the fact that most cases of absence are for a few days and SSP is not payable for the first three days. There is nothing to stop an employer paying full wages for any period of sickness. The employee is simply paid as if she or he were working and what is payable as SSP is reclaimed by deduction from payments to the Inland Revenue. However, the co-operative still has to keep the required records under the scheme, including dates of certificated sickness, the employees' qualifying days and SSP payments made.

A small co-operative wishing to offer generous long-term sick pay to its members in the form of payments of full or half wages would be well advised to consider taking out an insurance policy against this continued payment of wages. Such a policy, usually called permanent health insurance or sickness and accident insurance should not be confused with private health insurance schemes. What it means is that after a period of time the payment of wages to the sick employee would be taken over by the insurance policy. Unfortunately, such policies tend to be prohibitively expensive unless a period of several months elapses before the policy comes into effect.

Pensions

Everybody 'earns' their state pension through national insurance payments. The state pension currently consists of two elements — the basic pension and an earnings-related additional pension. The basic pension is the familiar one we hear about at Budget time and is now theoretically increased each November. There is a single person's pension and a married person's pension which is about sixty per cent higher. To qualify for a full basic pension, about ninety per cent of the years of your working life must be 'qualifying years' in terms of national insurance contributions. This means the equivalent of fifty-two contributions at the minimum earnings level. Anything less than ninety per cent qualifying years reduces the pension on a sliding scale. The problem with this as with other national insurance contribution-related benefits is that they increasingly give little advantage over social security benefits.

The additional pension is related to earnings over a twenty-year period and was introduced in April 1978. When somebody retires, a calculation is made of their twenty highest years of earnings and 1¼ per cent of this is payable as an annual pension. The calculation is complicated by adjustments for inflation and deductions for the equivalent of the national insurance minimum earnings level.

It should be remembered that it is always possible for the government to reduce the value of the basic state pension and the earnings-related element, either by a change in the law or by administrative action. It is significant that only a few years after its introduction, there is already talk that the earnings-related scheme is going to prove too expensive.

Like other employers, co-operatives wanting to offer their employees better pension provision have the choice of either contracting out of the state scheme or offering a 'ride-on-top' scheme to give further benefit. Generally speaking a contracted-out private scheme, although it involves a reduction in NI contributions, would not be possible except for very large groups. This is because any such scheme must have a system of benefits at least equivalent to the state additional pension and this would be prohibitively expensive.

A 'ride-on-top' scheme offers a pension in addition to the state pension (both basic and additional). The field of pension schemes is notoriously complex and the language used is a paragon of mystification, so specialist advice is needed. Contributions to the scheme can be made by the employer (the co-operative) and by the members as individuals. Normally the employer contributions would be a minimum of five per cent of gross wages. Individuals can get tax relief on contributions up to the equivalent of fifteen per cent of their gross wages.

It is possible to have a scheme which is self-administered, ie where operation and investment are totally under the control of the co-operative. For a small co-operative this is likely to be expensive and time-consuming so one is inevitably forced into having a scheme managed by an insurance company, which means there is no control over investments. In assessing schemes, the basic things to look at are the levels of contributions and benefits, administrative charges and investment performance. Then there is the question of additional benefits — dependants' pensions, life insurance etc. The question of transferability is also very important; in some cases if people change jobs the pension is either lost or frozen. Finally the question of discrimination between males and females should be looked at closely.

A pension scheme has now been developed specifically for workers co-operatives and some representation will be allowed for scheme members on the investment panel. Details can be obtained from local co-operative development agencies.

Disciplinary rules and procedures

For obvious reasons, industrial discipline can be a difficult area for co-operatives. Many people are attracted to working in co-operatives because of their disenchantment with the often archaic forms of authority and discipline existing in most workplaces. The lack of a hierarchical management structure can make it even easier to ignore what can be very painful problems. Yet the fact has to be faced that discipline (preferably self-discipline) is necessary if a co-operative is to function properly, both in business terms and as a democratic organisation. A co-operative can easily be destroyed if the problem of someone not keeping to agreed rules is not dealt with. The best protection of all is to have rules and procedures that are written down and known to everyone, particularly new employees. This is what the law demands anyway and it should not be forgotten that workers in co-operatives are employees and thus have the right to take their employer, the co-operative, to an industrial tribunal to claim unfair dismissal. The Act does not lay down the rules and procedures that an employer should have but there is an ACAS code of practice. This is written with hierarchical organisations in mind and therefore needs some adjustment to be suitable for a co-operative.

It is not necessary to have all the details of standards of working and personal behaviour written down, but it is essential that everything is fully discussed and agreed. It then becomes 'custom and practice'. However, there can be a problem for new employees, in that they are not so aware as older members of standards that may have become an accepted part of the working environment over a long period. A certain amount of this is transmitted in job interviews and job descriptions but it is important that new employees are actively introduced into the co-operative by induction sessions, 'twinning' with existing members and attending meetings.

The next thing is to establish a disciplinary procedure and a body responsible for carrying out this procedure. This should definitely be written down and entered in the co-operative's secondary rules. However, before a procedure can be used, there is a particular problem in co-operatives of how disciplinary matters are to be raised. If there is an appointed manager or a rotated co-ordinator, then it is less of a problem since the institution of disciplinary procedures could be part of their job description. In a small co-operative, running itself efficiently through weekly meetings, it can be difficult to raise the question of disciplining a member, particularly if she or he is sitting in the same meeting. If this means the problem is discussed outside the meeting when the member concerned is not there, we can already see the democratic basis of the co-operative breaking down.

There is obviously a strong case for an elected person or sub-committee within the co-operative to be responsible for instituting disciplinary procedures. The first responsibility would be to try to sort things out without recourse to formal procedures. Some co-operatives may feel strongly that this should be done in the full meeting of the co-operative and that it is essential that such problems are dealt with out in the open by everyone. This may well be suitable for some organisations but it is fair to say that our experience shows it to be disruptive and ineffective.

If it becomes necessary to institute formal procedures, there are various ground rules as to how these should operate:

- rules of conduct should be clear and known to all
- rules of procedure and who is responsible for carrying them out should also be clear and known to all
- the procedure should be reasonably speedy, within the constraints of proper investigation
- investigations of the facts surrounding each case should be carried out
- a written record should be kept

- the person concerned should have the right to present their case and to be represented or bring someone along with them
- there should be a right of appeal at each stage
- there should be no dismissal for a first offence except in the case of gross misconduct
- disciplinary warnings should be obliterated after an agreed period of time.

The procedure itself should follow these lines:

- **First stage — verbal warning**
  The individual should be told what to do about the situation. The warning should lapse after an agreed period, say one month.

- **Second stage — written warning**
  If the breach of discipline is repeated within the period of the previous warning, then the procedure should be repeated but this time with a written warning. Warning period three months.

- **Third stage — written warning**
  This time the individual should be warned in writing that a further breach will lead to dismissal. Warning period three months.

- **Final stage — dismissal**
  If the situation continues within the time limit of the previous warning, then the final stage should be dismissal. Such a decision should only be carried out by the whole co-operative in a general meeting·

The person concerned should have the right of appeal to the full co-operative at either a weekly or general meeting, with the possible exception of the first stage. The co-operative must not be frightened to allow trade union representatives to be involved; such representation is the fundamental right of any employee.

Gross misconduct is behaviour, such as theft or assault, which would make it impossible for the person concerned to remain working alongside other members. In such cases the co-operative can dismiss immediately or more properly suspend the person on full pay while an investigation is carried out. It does not apply to incidents taking place outside the workplace and not connected with the co-operative.

Co-operative members might well object that this disciplinary procedure takes too long and is too formal for dealing with someone who is clearly exploiting their fellow members by their behaviour or even threatening the future of the co-operative. This may be true in a small minority of cases but problems of discipline at work are hardly ever black and white. Although clear breaches of rules and clear culpability do exist, they are almost always surrounded by a mass of potentially mitigating factors and associated problems. There is almost certainly another side to the argument. The

47

individual involved may have all sorts of other problems, both personal and with the working group. In short, the breach of rules may be clear but it is probably a symptom of some other problem. In reality, except in cases of gross misconduct, it will be found that a timetable of the sort suggested here is needed before the irrevocable decision to dismiss is taken. The formality of the procedure is essential to protect the interests of both parties and does not prevent more informal attempts to sort things out going on at the same time.

Grievance procedure

As well as a disciplinary procedure which allows the co-operative as a whole to take action against an employee, there must be a system whereby individuals in the co-operative can take up complaints against other individuals or against decisions of the co-operative as a whole. As with disciplinary matters, one of the biggest difficulties in a co-operative is actually raising the problem.

One of the best ways of dealing with initial grievances and disputes is the 'third person' approach. The co-operative elects a complaints person who can be approached on a confidential basis by any aggrieved person and whose job it is to mediate between the individuals concerned or the individual and the manager and try to sort out the problem. If this works, it is not necessary to have the problem brought up before the committee of management. If the matter cannot be sorted out, then a more formal procedure similar to the disciplinary procedure should be adopted:

- **First stage**
Appeal to the named body responsible for dealing with grievances — either the co-operative meeting or a sub-committee. The matter should be properly investigated and a formal proposal made to resolve the problem. The individual concerned should have the right of representation by a trade union representative or another person if they so wish.

- **Second stage**
If the person is still not satisfied with the recommendations, she or he should have the right of appeal to an independent outside body. The government conciliation service ACAS would act in such a role but in the case of a co-operative, it might be better to involve other local co-operatives, the local CDA and local trade unions in forming an appeals panel. The decision of the appeals panel should be final.

All along it should be remembered that dealing with discipline and disputes can be a very damaging experience for a co-operative and it is not good enough to wait until something happens before working out procedures. They must be prepared and ready even if they are never used. Finally, however clear it is to the other members that an individual is in the wrong, his or her rights must always be respected and not be overruled by the collective power of the majority.

Dismissal

Since an employer/employee relationship exists in a co-operative, there is always the possibility of the dismissal of an employee and thus a claim of unfair dismissal being made to an industrial tribunal. One of the problems here is that the legal definition of dismissal is much wider than is commonly understood. Normally we consider being sacked as synonymous with dismissal but in fact all sorts of circumstances under which an employee leaves her or his job are legally defined as forms of dismissal. First we need to differentiate between circumstances which are regarded as dismissal and those that are not. Thereafter cases of dismissal can be considered fair or unfair. This question can be tested by an industrial tribunal.

The following circumstances are legally regarded as forms of dismissal, whether fair or unfair:

• **Termination of employment with or without notice**
This is what is commonly known as being sacked. In questions of whether such dismissal is fair or unfair, the legal minimum periods of notice or whatever extensions have been made in the contract of employment are of great importance, although they are not the only factor. Sacking on the spot without notice is known as summary dismissal. Warnings of dismissal do not constitute giving notice.

• **Refusal to renew a fixed term contract**
A fixed term contract is one which cannot be terminated by either side giving notice and which ends on a particular date. If such a contract ends and is not renewed, then a dismissal has taken place. In some circumstances, such as when the job the employee has been doing or a similar one still exists, there might be the basis for claiming that the dismissal was unfair. Depending on the period of the contract, some workers on fixed term contracts are not allowed to make claims to tribunals for unfair dismissal or redundancy pay and employers often attempt to use such contracts as a way of getting round the law. Co-operatives should beware of issuing fixed term contracts except in situations where they are genuinely necessary such as replacing someone on maternity leave or for initial probationary periods.

• **Redundancy**

• **Sacking after a strike or lock-out**
Strikes can and do occur in co-operatives. As happened in the Grunwick

dispute, an employer can protect himself from claims for unfair dismissal by sacking all those on strike.

- **Refusal to allow return to work after pregnancy**

If a woman has the right to return to her job and is refused re-employment on the stated date of return, this is a form of dismissal and the basis of a claim for unfair dismissal. More details are given in the section on **Maternity rights.**

- **Constructive dismissal**

This covers situations where an employee is forced into leaving by the actions of the employer. Even where an employee appears to have walked out or left of her or his own free will, there could still be a constructive dismissal. It usually occurs when the employer breaks important contractual obligations, such as making reductions in pay, increases in working hours or changes in the job without the agreement of the employee. It also includes cases of personal harassment. It would not normally apply when decisions had been properly taken by the democratic processes of the co-operative to make changes in contractual terms of employment.

All these are situations where a dismissal has taken place and that dismissal can be judged either fair or unfair. The following are circumstances where a dismissal is not considered to have taken place:

- where the employee agrees to be suspended
- where the employee leaves or resigns by mutual agreement
- where the company goes into liquidation
- 'frustration' of contract. This is when the very basis of the contract of employment is frustrated, eg the employee dies, is seriously disabled or imprisoned for a long time.

When an employee has been dismissed she or he has the right to claim unfair dismissal before an industrial tribunal. The law states that the employer must give the dismissed employee a written statement of the reasons for dismissal if she or he has been employed for more than six months. Applications for unfair dismissal must be made within three months of dismissal.

Some of the cases in which an industrial tribunal could judge that dismissal was unfair are

Redundancy

Although a redundant employee can claim redundancy pay, an employee can claim that the redundancy is unfair in various situations (see **Redundancy**).

Sex or race discrimination

It should be noted that the Sex Discrimination Act only applies to employers with more than five employees.

Trade union activities or membership

Dismissal on grounds of trade union activities or membership is automatically unfair.

There are considerable restrictions on employees' rights to make claims to tribunals and these have been increased by recent legislation. A full-time employee (sixteen hours per week or more) must have fifty-two weeks continuous service with the employer before the date of dismissal. This is extended to two years' continuous service if the employer has had fewer than twenty-one workers during that two-year period. Part-time workers (eight to fifteen hours per week) must have five years continuous service to make such claims. These restrictions do not apply in the case of claims against unfair dismissal on the grounds of trade union activities or membership or discrimination under the Race Relations Act or Sex Discrimination Act (see **Discrimination**).

At a tribunal, the employer must give reasons for the dismissal. In order to be judged fair, the employer must claim that the employee was dismissed on the grounds of:

* conduct and behaviour
* capability, skills or health
* qualifications relative to the position
* that continued employment would contravene a legal provision
* 'other substantial reason'.

In the event of a successful claim, the tribunal can order re-instatement or award compensation. In fact, tribunals are ineffective in defending workers' rights. Less than one claim in four is won, less than one per cent of cases result in re-instatement and awards are generally derisory. Whatever the outcome, however, in most cases it would be an indictment of the co-operative as an employer and a democratic organisation to be taken before an industrial tribunal.

Redundancy

As employees, members of the co-operative are entitled to payments when made redundant by a decision of the co-operative or in the event of the business winding up. Co-operatives can claim forty-one per cent of statutory payments from the government's redundancy fund. Since one of the prime purposes of a co-operative is to create democratically-controlled employment, redundancies should only be used as a last resort. All possible alternatives such as reductions in hours and voluntary redundancies should be considered before people are forced to give up their jobs. Under the Act, an employee has the right to reasonable amounts of paid time-off to look for other work or to arrange training during the period of notice leading up to redundancy.

The law requires employers to consult with recognised trade unions in the case of any redundancy. If ten or more workers are to be made redundant, the union must be consulted thirty days before the first sacking. If 100 or more workers are involved, the period is ninety days. There is a similar obligation to notify the Department of Employment of proposed redundancies. If consultations are not carried out, the trade union can make a claim on behalf of its threatened members to an industrial tribunal. If the Department of Employment is not notified, there is a danger that the co-operative could lose its right to claim rebates on redundancy payments. However, in liquidation and other such situations an employer can claim that special circumstances made consultations and notifications impractical.

In order to qualify for statutory redundancy pay, an employee must have two years' full-time service with the employer of sixteen hours a week or more or five years' service of between eight and fifteen hours per week. The awards are as follows:

18 to 21 years old: ½ week's pay per year of service.
22 to 40 years old: 1 week's pay per year of service.
41 to 64 years old: 1½ weeks' pay per year of service.

The maximum period is twenty years and there is a maximum weekly pay fixed by the government (currently £140 per week). Redundancy pay is not taxable and does not affect unemployment benefit. These are of course statutory minimums and can be improved by the co-operative.

There are a wide range of measures that a co-operative can consider as an alternative to enforced redundancies apart from the more obvious ones:

- are there goods and services which the co-operative purchases from outside or sub-contracts out which could be produced or performed within the co-operative?
- would re-training and job rotation help retain jobs?
- is the apparent need for redundancies a sign that the co-operative should be looking at new products or services rather than cutting back?
- has everything been done in the way of reducing hours, sharing work and ending overtime?
- would short-time working be a suitable alternative?
- have all sources of government or other help to protect jobs been investigated?

If enforced redundancies are inevitable, then the co-operative will have to have an agreed system for carrying them out. The usual one is 'last-in, first-out'.

Insolvency

Most co-operatives are new start-up small businesses. The failure rates for such businesses are very high, particularly in times of recession, although it seems from available statistics that co-operatives have a better survival rate. In view of this we should not be surprised if some co-operatives are forced into closure. The members of a co-operative are strongly protected in the event of liquidation. The limited liability of the co-operative means they are not personally responsible for the debts as long as they have traded in a proper way and not criminally built up debts knowing that there was no possibility of paying them. As employees they are protected if the co-operative is forced to close without being able to fulfil its obligations as an employer.

The state redundancy fund will guarantee the following payments, which have to be claimed through the liquidator or receiver:

- statutory redundancy pay
- statutory maternity pay
- arrears of pay up to eight weeks
- payment in lieu of notice to statutory minimum
- holiday pay up to six weeks

These payments are to a maximum of £140 per week per employee. If money is still owed to an employee over and above these amounts, the employee counts as a preferential creditor along with public authorities.

Maternity and paternity rights

If co-operatives are serious about offering people a better working environment, then one area they must tackle is provision for people with young children. Legal provision is minimal and at the very least improvements can be made in the flexibility of the system at little or no cost to the co-operative. There are no legal rights to paternity leave or pay and recent legislation has cut back on maternity rights.

The rights of women workers who are pregnant are hedged around with restrictions and any co-operative ought to be able to improve on the legal minimums. The only basic right is for paid time off to attend ante-natal sessions. Theoretically under the Act no woman can be dismissed for being pregnant but the right to claim unfair dismissal is dependent on the length of service conditions that apply to all claims for unfair dismissal. The same applies to the right to be offered suitable alternative work if incapable of normal work during pregnancy. In order to be eligible for maternity leave and maternity pay, a pregnant woman must have completed two years' service of sixteen hours a week or more, or five years' service of between eight and sixteen hours per week. This service must have been completed by the eleventh week before confinement. The woman can then take maternity leave starting any time after the eleventh week before confinement and has the right to return to work at any time within twenty-nine weeks of the week of confinement. Maternity pay is due for the first six weeks of absence whether or not the woman intends to return to work. Maternity pay consists of nine tenths of normal weekly pay and can be reclaimed by the employer. The employee's social security maternity allowance is deducted from maternity pay. The right of return provisions have been made more difficult under recent legislation. Companies with fewer than five employees do not have to offer a woman her job back and notification must be given in writing by the woman of her intention to return.

Besides improving on these basic rights and making the arrangements more flexible, there are a variety of ways a co-operative may want to help those of its members with children or other dependants. Paid paternity leave is an obvious starter but other things to consider are adjustments to pay rates in terms of need, provision of on-site childcare facilities or at least babysitting allowances for evening or weekend meetings, and paid compassionate leave when someone has to look after a dependant.

Discrimination

There are a number of Acts which attempt to outlaw various aspects of discrimination in employment including the Sex Discrimination Act 1975, the Race Relations Act 1976, the Equal Pay Act 1970, the Rehabilitation of Offenders Act 1974 and the Disabled Persons Employment Acts 1944 and 1958. The legislation is strong in theory and intention but less effective in practice. Co-operatives need to ensure that their good intentions in this field are translated into positive policies to make sure that discrimination does not occur in recruitment or employment. Often the only way to do this is to adopt policies of positive discrimination in favour of disadvantaged groups. The first two Acts make it illegal to discriminate on grounds of sex or race in either recruitment or employment although the Sex Discrimination Act does not apply to employers of fewer than six workers. Redress for individuals who consider they have been discriminated against is by application to an industrial tribunal and none of the length of service conditions that apply in claims against unfair dismissal are necessary in such claims.

The Equal Pay Act demands that women are given equal pay for equal work. The Rehabilitation of Offenders Act attempts to prevent discrimination in recruitment and employment against those whose convictions are deemed to have lapsed. The widely-ignored Disabled Persons Acts demand that employers with a workforce of over twenty should have three per cent disabled people employed.

Some co-operatives are set up with the specific aim of providing jobs for women or ethnic minority groups. Many will want to follow policies of positive discrimination in one form or another. Ironically, positive discrimination in favour of disadvantaged minorities is itself in danger of falling foul of the laws. Great care needs to be exercised in the way such discrimination is publicly advertised. A co-operative cannot advertise openly for a 'black worker', although it could say that applications from black people would be welcome. If fewer than six people are employed then it is possible to advertise for a woman, but otherwise the same applies. Only in cases where there are 'genuine occupational reasons', such as in the acting profession, do these rules not apply. There are similar constraints on the membership rules of a co-operative, so it would not be possible to include in the conditions of membership that it was confined to one sex or ethnic group. In view of these problems, it is advisable for co-operatives to take specialist legal advice on the implications of various public positive discrimination policies in relation to job advertisements and co-operative rules.

Time off work

There are various statutory rights to time off work, some of which have already been mentioned:

- paid time off for ante-natal care
- paid time off for those under notice of redundancy to look for another job or arrange re-training
- time off without right to be paid for public duties including trade union activities and elections or appointment to bodies such as local councils, magistrates courts, etc.

It is well worth the co-operative giving some consideration to the question of what additional time off is acceptable and what should be paid, ie personal business, care of dependants, long weekends etc. If a system of individual application to meetings for time off is used, it is often difficult to say no and there is a tendency for precedents to be established which may mean the co-operative ends up allowing much more than it can afford or with too much disruption of production.

One problem with rules in this area is that they never cover the intricacies of each case but some sort of consensus is necessary. One way is to allow individuals a certain number of hours' or days' leave that they can use at their own discretion for necessary personal business or paid compassionate leave. This should obviously be with the agreement of whoever is responsible for work schedules.

Pay

There is a general obligation on employers to pay contractually agreed wages and salaries for work done. The employer is also responsible for making the correct tax and national insurance deductions from employees' pay and paying such deductions to the Inland Revenue together with employers' national insurance contributions. By law, each employee must be given an itemised pay statement with their wages. This must include the following information:

- gross pay
- fixed deductions such as trade union dues
- variable deductions such as tax, national insurance, etc.

Health and safety at work

There is a considerable amount of legislation designed to ensure the health and safety of people at work, but the system of enforcement and monitoring is inadequate and so the law is widely ignored and ineffective. People are often appalled when they see how widespread is the toll of industrial death, accident and disability caused by unsafe working conditions. This is precisely the type of issue that a new co-operative whose members have a strong sense of only being responsible to themselves can too easily ignore. When co-ops are set up, tight finances make the temptation to cut corners even stronger. It should be remembered that the risk of death or injury applies not only to the working members but also to members of the general public who come on to the premises.

The most recent legislation of a major kind is the Health and Safety at Work Act 1974. It is concerned with the health and safety at work of both employees and the general public, the control of dangerous materials and the control of pollution. Employers must ensure the proper safety of plant, machinery and tools, storage, handling and transport of materials, premises and exits and the working environment. They are also responsible for the provision of information and training. Any employer with more than five employees must issue a statement of policy, covering the organisation and arrangements for health and safety together with the name of a person responsible for these. A recognised trade union may appoint a safety representative. A co-operative could be taken to court for following unsafe practices and employees can sue the co-operative for negligence.

In a small co-operative, perhaps the most practical way of dealing with these issues is to appoint one of the members as a safety representative, from the very beginning, with the job of investigating the safety of machinery and premises, fire precautions, environmental health etc, making sure that any necessary improvements in safeguards are implemented and then ensuring that standards are kept up.

Trade unions

There is a good deal of flatulent talk about co-operatives and trade unions, most of it from people who want trade unions to give their backing to co-operatives but not to get too closely involved with them. In a capitalist society, trade unions are primarily defensive organisations, so it should not come as a surprise if they and their officials are sometimes suspicious of organisations that take a different stance. Similarly, it is quite understandable that some people working in co-operatives take the attitude that trade unions are not necessary in their workplace because ownership and control are in the hands of the employees anyway.

There are, however, a number of good reasons why co-operative members should join trade unions and the co-operative should welcome trade union activity and officially recognise a trade union in the workplace. Either way, trade union activity and membership cannot be banned in the co-operative. As employees, co-operative members who consider they have been discriminated against on the grounds of trade union activity or membership have the right to seek redress at an industrial tribunal. Furthermore there are no qualifications in terms of length of service for an employee making such claims.

As has been stressed throughout this handbook, in a co-operative you are not 'your own boss' in the traditional sense of the self-employed. Because the co-operative is a legal entity, there is an employer (the co-operative) and employees (the working members and non-members). In terms of employment law, the fact that the employees control the employer is largely irrelevant and the relations are the same as between a traditional employer and employees. So there are responsibilities and rights on both sides and in structural terms there is room for the performance of most if not all traditional trade union functions.

Even in a small co-operative, a trade union organisation within the workplace can play a valuable role in policy making, particularly with regard to pay and conditions. As we stated, the members are both employers and employees. The committee of management or weekly meeting of the co-operative represents the employer or management side of this and it can be useful to have separate trade union meetings where members consider things from the point of view of employees. This applies not only to current questions but perhaps more importantly to the long-term planning of the co-operative.

The existence of a trade union organisation and of elected shop stewards can help to protect the interests of individuals and minority groups among the members and also the probationary workers who are not yet members of the co-operative and are in a potentially very vulnerable position. This role can be particularly important during disciplinary and grievance proceedings and in situations where redundancies are being considered.

Trade union members in a co-operative can play a valuable part in a wide range of union activity. This may also have internal benefits. Members should know what the 'going rate' of wages and conditions is in their industry and what other workers are attempting to achieve. This will help the co-operative avoid self-exploitation and under-cutting of workers in other similar workplaces. It is also essential, if the co-operative wants to offer good wages and conditions to its members, that it is not under-cut by other firms offering much worse conditions. One of the most practical ways of doing something about this is for co-operative members to be involved in their trade unions at local and national level. There have been moves recently to set up special trade union branches for co-operative workers, irrespective of industry. Generally speaking, this seems to be the wrong approach. From every point of view, it is more appropriate for co-operative workers to belong to and be active in the trade unions for their industry. Otherwise there is a danger of trade union membership becoming a mere token and the ghettoisation of workers co-operatives in the trade union movement. The common interests of workers in different co-operatives can best be dealt with through joint trade union committees.

Finally, it should not need pointing out that co-operatives are not and cannot be islands in the rest of society and must have a wider perspective than purely their internal affairs. In this respect, co-operatives have always shared common aims and traditions with the trade union and labour movements.

Calvert's Press – a case study

'A producer co-op which is an economic failure is automatically a social failure. A producer co-op which is solely an economic success is of no social interest.'
*Antoine Antoni, 'The co-operative way'**

These words spring to mind when thinking of Calvert's Press in retrospect. Calvert's is anything but an economic success, yet it has nevertheless survived its first six years. So it has not been a failure either, although it has been on the brink more than once and recovered itself. In the course of its struggle against economic failure, the members of the co-op have had to resolve social as well as financial problems. Over the last few years questions of staff relations, conditions of work, terms of employment, job satisfaction, turnover of people, commitment, responsibility, and so forth have always been high up on our agenda. They are inextricably tied up with the financial and commercial side of the business. This case study of Calvert's Press concentrates on these aspects and considers what bearing they have had upon its precarious economic development.

Origins and aims

Calvert's Press was formed in 1977 with the aim of providing a comprehensive design, typesetting, and printing service to a primarily non-commercial market. Its origins lie in a dispute that occurred within another long since dissolved printing company in London which described itself as a co-operative. For the seven workers who left to start Calvert's, this was a vital aspect of their employment there. But in fact, ownership was in the hands of the boss. The justification for its 'co-operative' tag, was based on a facade of democracy within the firm and its liberal and non-commercial service to the 'arts'. The motivation, one suspects, was more to provide a 'soft' image for the market it sought out—one largely similar to Calvert's existing clientele— and to engineer an invidious form of exploitation over the employees under the guise of co-operative principles. In practice, of course, the crucial powers to make decisions about hiring and firing, wage levels, investment, planning etc were outside the workers' control. The moral and political opposition of the shop-floor workers to the regime was to

*The co-operative way: workers co-ops in France, Spain and Eastern Europe ICOM Co-Publications 1983

provide the catalyst which led to the inception of Calvert's Press as a *real* co-operative, and a determination not to compromise those ideals. They felt their position was even worse than in a conventional printing company, where at least the unionised wage-earners are under no illusions about where they stand. So with a leap of the imagination, an unwavering belief in co-operative principles and a few pounds scraped together by the founder members, Calvert's was born in the spring of 1977. There was barely anything to begin with beyond the commitment of the members and a few hundred pounds' worth of equipment.

The seven founder members agreed upon a minimum set of conditions for its operation. The company would be constituted under the full ICOM model rules for a common ownership co-operative; it should have a unionised workforce; it would pay at least the agreed union minimum wage and progress as quickly as possible to the industry average; the administration of the co-operative should be fully accountable and democratic, providing open access to the financial affairs of the company; and day-to-day production control should be in the hands of the shop-floor workers.

The early years

Operating from hand-to-mouth the co-operative battled through the first two years. The main pre-occupation was simply to get the work done efficiently, reliably, obtaining the best quality from poor machinery, and at a price the customers could afford without Calvert's making a loss. The large measure of agreement established between the workers at the beginning over the principles involved provided a powerful inertia which maintained the social cohesiveness of the collective during this fragile period. But this environment also came under inevitable criticism for stifling the initiative and aspirations of new workers. The ways in which things were done were often seen as being ordained on stone tablets and no longer subject to change despite the shifting complexion of the membership. The problem was to grow. One by one, founder members were burning themselves out or had other plans which could not be put off forever. By August 1979 only three remained. Recruitment of staff for the second generation of Calvert's Press was becoming an urgent problem. During 1978–79, five new workers came and went—some in unhappy circumstances. Commitment alone was obviously not sufficient to hold people and this was anxiously recognised.

This underlying issue of securing workers who could bring both a sufficient level of skill and experience to their job and a commitment to and aptitude for collective self-management was fundamental to the policy-making debate from then onwards. Calvert's was no longer its founder-members, with their motivation and reasons for doing things. The future would depend upon what the enterprise could offer to new members as much as it had hitherto depended upon what the members could offer to the enterprise. A choice was faced between continuing a process of cautious growth, hampered by old and troublesome machinery, relying enormously upon the commitment and flexibility of the workforce, and restricted to a market which was loyal and sympathetic to the Press despite production problems. Or alternatively, the main priority would be to increase efficiency and productivity, plan new investment, raise wages significantly, and above all secure the financial well-being of the business in order to provide social benefits that would meet the needs and desires of the workers. But at what cost to the co-operative principles so doggedly fought for? What room would be left for job rotation, sharing of skills, and providing employment opportunities for people, particularly women, otherwise hard to get within the print. For efficiency's sake, how much would the workers control over production schedules be sacrificed?

In theory, of course, there is not a clear cut choice to be made between such alternatives—the commercial as against the co-operative. The goal is always to seek a fusion of the two—economic *and* social success. The issues, however, were polarized and distorted in practice through an event which took place during the winter of 1979–80 which was to have a destabilizing, but ultimately clarifying effect upon Calvert's. A proposal had emerged in August 1979 to amalgamate with another co-operatively run business in London — Spider Web Offset. It was not at that time a common ownership co-op. They had more money, better machinery, a greater level of skill, and a seemingly different goal: simple commercial success was perceived to be their over-riding purpose. The arguments were fought over passionately. For some, largely the newest crop of people at Calvert's, this was without doubt the way forward. For others it was a dangerous threat to the identity of Calvert's Press and the uncompromised principles it had of what co-operative self-management meant. Calvert's believed that overtime should only be paid for with time off, not money—people should not have to work overtime, they said. Spider Web believed in top-down production control for efficiency's sake. Committees and working-parties were the best way to decide things whereas for Calvert's, general meetings were paramount. The arguments were exaggerated, the discussion divisive. Fundamentals were at stake.

For Calvert's, the whole affair was disastrous. As the amalgamation debate wore on, some people left in dismay, others were reluctantly won over, until eventually compromises were reached and the project seemed feasible. But then Spider Web called it off. They had discovered that we were a financial mess. And indeed we were. The very problems which some at Calvert's saw the amalgamation solving, albeit probably wrongly, had been continually growing. Demoralisation and uncertainty had been taking their toll on production and finances.

New directions

Six months later, cash flow troubles nearly bankrupted Calvert's. Those intervening months turn out however to be amongst the most creative in its history. The cash shortage was the result of risk taking. Much of the sound thinking of the amalgamation idea had sunk in—the rest was positively rejected. An investment programme was hurriedly worked out and a morale-boosting, high quality and reliable press was purchased, enabling us to take on trade work from other printers. A new urgency possessed Calvert's which provided the context for working out the issues which a year earlier had been so problematic.

Shift work was instituted temporarily during the autumn of 1980. The problems of absenteeism, bad time-keeping, and overtime allowances repeatedly came up in meetings. However, they were to be firmly and realistically dealt with. Payment, an an alternative to time off in lieu, was permitted in recognition of the inevitability of overtime working. It was however emphasised that no worker should be under an obligation from the administration, or elsewhere, to do it. That rule remains intact and unchallenged today. The rights of occasional casual workers at Calvert's, which had become ambiguous, were clarified at this time, preserving their right to attend meetings and be paid for this, but not to have a vote.

Looking back through the minutes of our meetings, it becomes clear that the co-operative ethos at Calvert's was sufficiently strong to make difficult and unpalatable decisions over social questions, in time of crisis, in order to make the business more efficient, productive and 'commercial' without sacrificing any principles of co-operation at all. At every level, the co-operative had to tighten itself up. The cash-flow situation was the danger signal: strict monitoring of credit-control and careful day-to-day juggling of the income and expenditure of funds was demanded. Meanwhile, the decisions that were being taken relating to employment matters and conditions of work were codified into a written contract of employment. This had been discussed many times before and as frequently deferred. The final document, although not unlike any other conventional contract, was largely the product of our experience.

Conditions of work

Two events in particular spurred on the formulation of this contract. In February 1981, Calvert's sacked a worker for the first time. The reason was absenteeism over a fairly long period. Whilst in the end there were no misgivings about the justification for this action, the collective nevertheless found it a difficult decision to make. A series of verbal and written warnings were given, in quite a proper manner, leaving the collective no choice but to issue the final letter of dismissal. We could not cope with the unreliability imposed upon the collective of a key production worker continually not turning up for work without apparent reason. It seemed difficult because there was a strong tendency to think that a co-operative shouldn't sack people, we should sort it out some other way. But in the end you have to, if the collective suffers intolerably, provided you have democratically worked out rules for doing it and you follow them to the letter. On a second occasion, a worker we had taken on was plainly not up to the job and we were worried about the loss of customers that was beginning to arise as a result. At the end of his probationary period we dismissed him, because there was not a majority in favour of giving the person full membership of the co-operative. Under our rules, the issue is simple: a worker may not remain as a non-member after the end of the probationary period—no membership, no job. That is the negative side. On the other hand, the terms and conditions of holidays, time off in lieu of overtime, freely decidable flexible hours of working, maternity, paternity and compassionate leave and sick pay and medical appointments, which are at least as good as anywhere in the industry, have been formulated and embodied in a written contract of employment. People benefit from the contract and at the same time it protects the collective livelihood of the co-operative against potentially difficult employment problems. There are probably too many co-operatives that do not have a clear contract of employment worked out, but in our experience, it is vital to provide an authority to refer to, if and when you get in difficulties. The co-operative, if it manages itself properly, will always be in control of and able to develop the contract.

The contract of employment is interesting, not because we have one—all co-ops should—but because its eventual formulation, after several years of discussion, was the result of seeking to implement a definite, if not totally explicit, policy regarding the future direction Calvert's needed to take. It was acknowledged that it was important to establish an existence for the company that was independent of the energy and commitment of its members. Simply because those things, whilst absolutely essential at the beginning, cannot sustain the life of the co-op for ever. Indeed, ultimately it has to be the other way around—the point of working in a co-operative has to be at least to satisfy the economic needs of its workers without draining them in the process. As well as being a very practical document it represents the contradiction present in all co-ops between its members as workers and as managers. On the one hand it protects the collective against the effects of individual problems within it, whilst simultaneously preserving the rights and benefits of individuals within the collective. In Calvert's case it was part of a general process over the last three years which included heavy capital investment in the project, both to make the work more satisfying, skill-enhancing, and less arduous (in order to reduce the level of staff turnover arising from exhaustion) and also to provide future staff stability as insurance against the long-term risks associated with heavy borrowing.

By no means everything relevant to the social organisation of work and employment is contained in this document. Before concluding I ought to mention briefly a few other features of the way we run things. Very early on in our history it was decided to institute a form of 'clocking in'. We simply use a book in which people write down the time they arrive at work and the time they leave. At the end of the week, everybody calculates the total hours they have worked. It has two functions: it enables each person to know how much time off or payment they are due for extra hours worked, and it permits the collective to see whether everybody is working sufficient hours, or the hours they say they do, or most usually, if it is too many, whether to take remedial action and take on extra staff.

Job rotation is an aspect of life which co-ops are frequently pre-occupied with. Except in terms of people requesting a transfer from one department to another, subject to vacancies being available, we do not apply any system of regular rotation. The reason is simple: the level of skill demanded of each person requires that each be specialised in their own job, which can only be developed by concentrating on it. Our experience of rotating work stations in the past has been that it is disorientating and dissatisfying.

Finally, our method of staff recruitment has changed in the last two years. There is no sense in pretending that a collective of a dozen people can all take an equal part in the selection of job applicants. Our practice is to sift the applications collectively, draw up a short-list and give everyone a chance to speak to the applicants informally but delegate the detailed interviewing to a small group and accept their recommendation if there is a consensus of opinion. We feel that only a small group conducting interviews can reach the depth necessary to make a sensible choice as well as enabling the applicants to feel relaxed and open about themselves.

Strengthening co-operative principles

All the social developments, the tensions and their gradual resolution that have taken place at Calvert's have happened in the context of an economic history. Calvert's began life chronically undercapitalised and nearly paid the penalty for such an undertaking. In the past three years we have quadrupled the level of capital investment in the business, largely through expensive high-risk loan finance. Wages have risen by forty per cent in that time and sales have doubled. Also the rate of staff turnover has fallen dramatically despite a subsequent protracted period of extreme financial anxiety. Perhaps the balance between what people have to put in to the place to keep it going and what they get from it is evening out. There are many dissatisfactions still and much development work to be done, but an economic strategy of increasing commercialisation is in full-throw. Yet far from meaning the abandonment of principles of co-operation, it enables them to be strengthened. The co-operative adopts more and more a life of its own, independent of the vicissitudes of its members, but it also begins to feel more like a place where you might want to work for a long while, where you could support a family, where you could regard it as an ordinary job if you wish (only one better than most because you are in control of its conditions) but where also, if you have the energy and desire for it, you can as part of a collective make of it what you want.

Tony Hodgson
Calvert's

Trylon – a case study

In the beginning . . .

Trylon is perhaps best described as a common ownership rather than the more usual 'co-operative' because, while undoubtedly a co-operative, it remains almost the last of the pioneering examples of co-ops established before cheap, simple model rules became available. Trylon has been described as having the structure of a living dinosaur; but although the structure is complex, the members do understand it. It was established as a common ownership around 1968, one of the 'second wave' of concerns largely inspired by the legendary Ernest Bader. It was, however, not until 1973 that the complex legal struggle to produce a constitution was finally resolved. The lack of model rules for co-ops at that time meant that solicitors, accountants and the Charity Commissioners were forced to go back to basic principles in advising on the legal structure. This proved very time consuming and costly. We eventually succeeded and still retain the original two-tier structure whereby Trylon Community Ltd, a registered charity with trustees, holds the shares both of Trylon and a recently acquired smaller subsidiary, Alger-Sanders Ltd. The employees of both these concerns are the members of the holding company and we thus fully comply with the first commandment of any co-operative which is that it should be 'owned and controlled by those who work in it'.

Trylon is small and probably likely to stay that way. Currently, there are eleven full-time workers and five part-time workers. Six of the members have worked for Trylon for over ten years and thus represent a rare concentration of co-operative experience. The value of this experience hits us afresh every time a new person joins the co-operative.

In the early seventies, craft in schools was undergoing a revolution. Plastics and modern materials were slowly being appreciated in their own right as supplements or alternatives to traditional wood and metal. Trylon was able to supply, develop and teach the techniques of using these new materials and is still adding materials and projects to what is now an accepted part of the school craft syllabus. We pioneered the use of glass fibre, resins and plastics in craft education and are now a major distributor to educational establishments, craft shops, museums, industry and the general public.

The purchase of Alger-Sanders Ltd last year enabled us to supplement raw materials with a range of tools, equipment and coated cutters for the glass fibre industry giving the group a combined turnover approaching £½ million.

Dare we break the tablets of stone?

All enterprises need a statement of philosophy, and Trylon adopted such a statement early in its life. The hammering out of this preamble to the constitution gave rise to many problems and arguments. Despite this, it still remains the key to everything Trylon stands for. The preamble states that as well as being an economic enterprise, Trylon is a community of people concerned with the quality of life at work, and that:

- . . . a part of any surplus arising from our work should be shared amongst us and an equal part spent on people and projects outside the company (this has been changed several times to a rule basing the payments on a proportion of salary thus making our social objectives independent of profit).
- we will not supply products which we believe would be likely to be used specifically for war purposes.
- we hope to influence and help the formation of other similar working communities . . .
- we should meet regularly to discuss and share the decisions which affect our work. We wish to build a self-governing community of like-minded people acknowledging our dependence on a transcendent creative power outside ourselves.

The dilemmas we face in trying to fulfil the almost saintly demands of this preamble are not unheard of in long-established common ownerships. The preamble was written by the founders, all of whom are no longer members. Should we retain it as 'tablets of stone' or should we admit that things and people change and that this should be reflected in the preamble? The debate continues.

Membership and trustees

To maintain a good structure in a co-op requires a series of checks and balances. Trylon has built in plenty. Having been selected as a new employee, which is in itself somewhat arduous, everyone is expected to serve a trial period before applying for membership and membership is conditional upon acceptance of the preamble and acceptance by the other members. Even when someone has been accepted into membership, there is another built-in check, namely that everyone must re-apply for membership each year. This means that nobody is 'in for life' and it gives the opportunity, which is painfully difficult to grasp, to reassess each individual's contribution to the co-op as a whole. Operating this rule has proved very difficult. While on the very odd occasion a re-application has been rejected, the members remain dissatisfied with a method that usually gives a unanimous election without debate.

Next we have the trustees, a group comprising some members of the co-operative and some people from outside. They have limited formal powers as trustees of the charitable holding company, but their prime task is acting as 'guardians of the constitution' and, more importantly, filling the role of advisors and arbitrators in relation to the co-op. They do not, however, have any powers of veto over the members. From time to time, problems do arise which the membership are unable to stand back from and in these circumstances, the trustees can prove immensely useful. Other established co-ops are beginning to recognise the need for such a group and our system is likely to be copied in the near future.

What do you do with the founder?

Because it has been around a long time and has outlived many of its contemporaries, Trylon has tried out most systems of democratic control and decision making and is indeed still trying. Unlike many co-ops, however, it fairly soon overcame the classic dilemma which many new co-ops have not yet thought about; namely, finding a painless way of getting the founders to release control. In 1968, one of the founding entrepreneurs and a self-confessed authoritarian managing director was appointed. Whilst some would argue that managers in a co-op are a contradiction in terms, many would contend that this type of individual is vital in the early years. They can also prove somewhat difficult to remove! By 1974, Trylon had established an immensely strong trading base and sound democratic structures. To his credit, the managing director decided to move on, initially to serve the common ownership movement and later to create another and very different type of co-operative. Trylon was thus able to appoint its 'second generation' general manager. The system we used has been recognised as the established method of managerial appointment in co-ops.

The members' meeting

The prime decision-taking body at Trylon is the weekly general meeting of the members of Trylon Community Ltd. Officers are elected annually by the full-time workers and everyone has filled these roles, apart from the general manager, over the years. All major decisions and some very minor matters are dealt with at these meetings and as to their effectiveness we can only say that 'when it's good, it's very, very good and when it's bad, it's awful!'

At best, consensus is reached quite naturally after a debate of the various options with most people making positive contributions and amendments. At worst, we limp forward with four people in favour of a certain decision, one against and six abstentions. If we analysed these cases, we would probably find that not all the information the members would have liked was made available or perhaps sometimes members would have preferred the manager to make the decision.

We are always seeking changes in methods to improve meetings and recently introduced a 'seven day rule' which gives any member the right to block any decision for seven days even if carried by an overwhelming majority. Notice that the rule is being applied must be given immediately after the meeting. The rule gives a useful period for further reflection before the item is discussed and finally resolved at the next meeting. This rule has been used perhaps only four times in five years but it remains an essential check.

To ensure that the widest range of topics are regularly considered, the agenda for the weekly meeting is split into five areas:

People covers any aspect of welfare, new appointments, salaries, holidays etc.

Social projects covers consideration of appeals and projects outside the company. We currently allocate one quarter of the average member's salary to social objectives.

Economic tasks allows for discussion of any aspect of the company's trading activities, new products, customer complaints, budgets, monthly sales figures, cash flow etc.

Political tasks covers reports of activities taking place to promote common ownerships and our involvement or otherwise.

Warehouse stock is a formal item which allows for reports about what products from our catalogue are either low or out of stock.

It's really a question of style!

The manager's role in the decision making process cannot be ignored. The present manager continues to promote the concept of the manager as a servant/leader. This sometimes proves both difficult for the members to understand and for the manager to maintain. Nevertheless the members accept that a good range of decisions are the manager's undisputed area of activity such as pricing, cash flow, budgets and, perhaps, discipline. The manager also largely controls what items get onto the agenda of the weekly meetings although the open structure means that any member has access to an arsenal of facts with which to initiate a debate. However, the existence of a manager raises a number of issues about how decisions should be taken. On the one hand, the manager can present all the available facts to the meeting and then describe all the options open. This inevitably means that the manager puts forward a number of options which are not really viable and can lead to accusations of management waffling.

On the other hand, the manager can present all the facts, boldly state the way forward and ask for support for this view. This will probably lead to accusations of authoritarian behaviour. Two decisions taken recently at Trylon illustrate these different approaches.

The members wanted to reduce their working week and the manager put forward a range of options including reduced hours, flexi-time, half day closing etc. None of these was taken up. Instead the discussion threw up an idea which fitted our circumstances exactly. We now each take a half day off every fortnight on an agreed rota basis. Apart from minor adjustments such as controlling the number of Friday afternoons members are permitted, the system has worked well and shows group decision taking at its best.

In 1982 in the middle of the recession, Trylon had been able to maintain full employment but things were not easy. We desperately needed to increase turnover and members were very worried. The opportunity of purchasing a small subsidiary arose and the manager decided to proceed with negotiations, only placing the matter before the members at quite an advanced stage, giving members only the final decision on whether to proceed with the purchase or back out. True democrats might consider this wrong but it did work and the move is proving very successful.

The above are both examples of democratic decision making in practice. It's sometimes frustrating and things can go wrong but the difference is that it's *our* decision and its success or failure can only be placed at our door. None of us can say 'It's all *their* fault'.

Michael Angerson
Trylon

Appendix 1   Employment calculations

Most employment rights depend on qualifying factors—periods of continuous service, normal working hours and a week's pay. The basic calculations are fairly straightforward but individual cases can often be hedged around with all sorts of complexities. It is impossible to go into full details here but the appendix aims to explain how the basic calculations are made.

Right	Qualifying service	Minimum number of hours
Statement of terms and conditions	13 weeks	16 hours per week (or between 8–16 hours for 5 years)
Maternity pay and right to return	2 years by 11th week before confinement	16 hours per week (or between 8–16 hours for 5 years)
Notice of termination	1 month	16 hours per week (or between 8–16 hours for 5 years)
Written reasons for dismissal	6 months	16 hours per week (or between 8–16 hours for 5 years)
Claims for unfair dismissal	1 year 2 years for employers with no more than 20 employees	16 hours per week (or between 8–16 hours for 5 years)
Redundancy pay	2 years	16 hours per week (or between 8–16 hours for 5 years)

Normal working hours Normal working hours are defined by contract, whether written, verbal or implied. Usually they are the hours worked before overtime is payable, although fixed overtime may be counted as part of normal hours.

A week's pay For workers on a fixed wage or salary, a week's pay is the normal payable for a period of normal weekly working hours. Where pay varies, it is calculated on the average weekly or hourly pay over the last twelve weeks.

71

Continuous service Normally only weeks in which employment is of sixteen hours a week or more count towards continuous service. Employees who have worked for at least eight but less than sixteen hours a week qualify after five years.

If the contract is for sixteen hours or more but is varied to be less than sixteen but more than eight, then those weeks still count up to a maximum of twenty-six weeks. Over twenty-six weeks the continuity is not broken but the weeks cease to count towards continuous service. Once service qualifications have been established, then they are retained unless contract hours drop below eight. Continuous service is also broken if the employee stops working for the employer except in the following circumstances:

- absence through sickness as long as the employee returns within twenty-six weeks
- pregnancy, as long as the employee returns within the statutory time
- a temporary stoppage or where the employee is considered to be continuing in employment
- when employees are taken back on after dismissal, either by application to a tribunal or otherwise, the missing period counts towards continuous service
- the same applies to employees who are made redundant but re-engaged within four weeks
- days lost during strikes or lock-outs do not count towards continuous service but do not break continuity
- sometimes continuity is not broken even if there is a new employer. This is basically when the business and the contracts of employment are taken over from the old employer by the new one.

Appendix 2 Specimen contract of employment

This specimen contract is intended purely as a guideline to suitable terms and conditions of employment for a co-operative. New co-ops will often not be able to afford the full range of benefits, but can use these guidelines as something to aim for. You may feel that some or all of the conditions are inadequate and need changing—or changes may have to be made to reflect different circumstances in different co-ops. In some cases, figures are given as a general guide (eg holidays), in others they have been left blank (rate of pay) for you to decide. It should be borne in mind that in some areas, legal minimum conditions of employment apply (eg periods of notice, maternity pay).

---

1 **Name of employer** _____

2 **Name of employee** _____

3 **Date of commencement of employment** _____

4 **Job title.** You are employed as a _____

You are also expected to participate in the management of the co-operative and carry out other duties as directed by the management committee.

5 **Pay.** The rate of pay is £_____ per month/week subject to deductions for tax and national insurance. Overtime is paid at £_____ per hour.

6 **Method of payment.** Payment is made by cheque monthly/weekly in arrears.

7 **Hours of work.** Full time employees—thirty-eight hours per week, between the hours of ———— Monday to Friday, with a one-hour lunch break. In addition, all workers who are members of the co-operative attend all management committee and general meetings for which they are paid at the hourly rate. Overtime done at the direction of the management committee is paid at the agreed rate for hours worked over and above these.

8 **Paid holidays.** Twenty-five days plus all public holidays per working year. Holidays may only be taken after appropriate notice has been given to the management committee or other authorised person. The holiday year begins on January 1st and holidays may only be carried over into the following year by application to the management committee. For periods of

less than a year, holiday entitlement is on a pro-rata basis. When an employee leaves, accrued holidays will be paid on a pro-rata basis.

9 **Illness and sick pay.** Each employee is entitled to full pay (less any statutory sick pay or other benefits) during a period of illness, up to a maximum of _____ weeks per annum. This will be followed by a period of half pay for a further _____ weeks. A medical certificate must be produced for periods of sickness longer than seven consecutive days.

10 **Absence and leave.** Each employee is entitled to ____ visits per year to doctors/dentists/family planning clinics etc during paid working time. Except in cases of emergency, such visits should be notified in advance to the management committee

11 **Parental leave and pay.** Provided that one year's continuous service has been completed, a female employee is entitled to receive maternity pay and to return to her job after the birth of the child. A medical certificate must be provided giving the expected date of birth. She must continue to be employed by the co-operative until eleven weeks before the expected date of birth.

Maternity pay: ____ weeks' full pay, less any maternity allowance or any other benefits, to be paid from the time leave commences.

Maternity leave: provided four weeks' notice is given in writing, the employee has the right to return to her job within a period of one year from leaving.

Time off: reasonable paid time off will be given for attendance at ante-natal clinics.

Paternity leave: male employees are entitled to ____ weeks' paid paternity leave at the time of the birth of a dependant child. Four weeks' notice must be given of the period to be taken.

12 **Pensions.** The co-operative will pay the equivalent of five per cent of the salary of employees who are members of the co-operative as employer's contributions into the co-operative's pension scheme.

13 **Trade union.** All employees of the co-operative are expected to join the appropriate trade union, the _____

14 **Probation and membership.** All new employees have a three-month probationary period. At the end of this period, and before six months of employment have been completed, all employees working more than ten hours per week must have applied for and been accepted into membership of the co-operative. New employees undergoing a probationary period are issued with a three-month fixed term contract, which can be renewed for one further three-month period if they have not yet applied for or been accepted into membership of the co-operative. Except in cases of

redundancy, membership of the co-operative will normally be given to any employee who has successfully completed her/his probationary period. Decisions on membership are taken at general meetings of the co-operative. Ex-employees of the co-operative who are re-employed may, at the discretion of the management committee, be exempted from the probationary period. All employees who are not members of the co-operative have the same conditions of employment as members, except that there is:

- no requirement to attend management meetings
- no maternity and paternity rights above statutory minimums
- no participation in co-operative pension schemes.

Where an application to become a member of the co-operative has been turned down, the employee has the right to a written explanation.

15 **Disciplinary procedure.** The following procedure is carried out if there are complaints about the conduct, attendance, time-keeping or job performance of any employee. The complaint must be put before the co-operative's disciplinary sub-committee. Investigations will be made fully, but as quickly as possible. The employee concerned has the right to present their case and to be represented or bring someone along with them. A written record will be kept. At each stage there is a right of appeal to the management committee. Warnings lapse after fixed periods of time at each stage. There is no dismissal for first offences, except in the case of gross misconduct. If the complaints are found to be justified:

First stage—verbal warning. The employee will be told what to do about the situation. The warning will lapse after one month.

Second stage—written warning. If the complaint persists, within the period of the previous warning, the procedure will be repeated, This time with a written warning. The warning will lapse after three months.

Third stage—written warning. At this stage the employee is warned in writing that a further breach of discipline will lead to dismissal. The warning will lapse after three months.

Fourth stage—dismissal. If there is a further breach of discipline within the period of the previous warning, the co-operative may decide, at a general meeting of all members, to dismiss the employee concerned.

16 **Grievance procedure.** This procedure is to be followed if any employee feels a grievance against any other employee, elected officers of the co-operative or decisions of the co-operative as a whole.

- S/he should raise the matter with the elected complaints person who will do her/his best to resolve the matter
- If no solution can be found, the employee should put her/his grievance to the sub-committee of the management committee, which will investigate the matter, hear representations from the people involved and

make a formal proposal for its solution. The employee has the right to be represented or to bring someone along with them.

- If the aggrieved person is still not satisfied, there is a right of appeal to the agreed outside, independent arbitration body. The decision of this body is binding on all parties.

17 **Notice of leaving.** Periods of notice for employees who are members of the co-operative are as follows. The same notice must be given by both employees and by the co-operative as employer:

Four weeks plus one week for every year of completed continuous service, up to a maximum of twelve weeks.

Further Reading

The workers co-operative handbook
Peter Cockerton and Anna Whyatt
ICOM Co-Publications 1984
A general and wide ranging introduction

Work aid: business management for co-operatives and community enterprises
Tony Naughton
Beechwood College 1981
A simple introduction to financial planning, accounts etc.

Employment law affecting worker co-operatives
Jim Brown
Beechwood College 1982
A short booklet dealing specifically with employment matters

Workers co-operatives: jobs and dreams
Jenny Thornley
Heinemann Educational Books 1981
An account of the historical and political aspects of workers co-operatives

Under new management
Tony Eccles
Pan Books 1981
The fascinating story of KME, one of the 'rescue' co-ops of the 1970s

The co-operative way: worker co-ops in France, Spain and Eastern Europe
ICOM Co-Publications 1983
Three papers on co-operative organisation in other European countries. Antoine Antoni's paper giving practical advice on self-management in French co-operatives is particularly useful.

Rights at work
Jeremy McMullen
Pluto Press 1983
A comprehensive manual on employment law written for trade unionists.

Information packs

How to form an industrial co-operative
ICOM

How to set up a worker co-operative
National CDA

How to start a co-operative
Beechwood College

Starting a workers co-operative
Lambeth CDA

Local co-operative development agencies in England and Wales

London

Brent CDA
192 High Road
London NW10
01 451 3777

Croydon CDA
99 London Road
Croydon
Surrey

Ealing CDA
Charles House
Bridge Road
Southall
Middlesex
01 574 4724

Greenwich Employment Resource Unit
311 Plumstead High Street
London SE18
01 310 6695

Hackney Co-operative Developments
16 Dalston Lane
London E8
01 254 3743

Hammersmith and Fulham Community Enterprise Development Agency
Bishop Creighton House
Lillie Road
London SW6
01 381 4446

Islington CDA
326–328 St Paul's Road
London N1
01 226 2783

Kingston CDA
Clarence Chambers
Fairfield West
Kingston
Surrey
01 549 9159

Lambeth CDA
460 Wandsworth Road
London SW8
01 720 1466

Lewisham CDA
38 Forestholme Close
London SE23
01 699 7508

Newham CDA
55 West Ham Lane
London E15
01 519 2377

Southwark CDA
135 Rye Lane
London SE15
01 732 9777

Waltham Forest CDA
160 High Street
London E17
01 520 4621

Wandsworth Enterprise Development Agency
Unity House
High Street
London SW18
01 870 2165

Westminster, Kensington and Chelsea CDA
37-39 Great Marlborough Street
London W1

South

Avon CDA
96 Stokes Croft
Bristol

Brighton Area CDA
c/o 17 Ditchling Rise
Brighton
0273 692664

Guildford CDA
c/o GAUPC
Old Police Station
3A Leapale Road
Guildford
Surrey
0483 33942

Midlands

Birmingham CDA
Bridge House
Bull Ring Centre
Smallbrook
Queensway
Birmingham
021 643 3531

Black Country CDA
Lich Buildings
44 Queen's Square
Wolverhampton
0902 773506

Cambridge CDA
25 Gwydir Street
Cambridge
0223 60977

Coventry CDA
Unit 15
Arches Industrial Estate
Spon End
Coventry
0203 714078

Derbyshire CDA
3 The Strand Arcade
Derby
0332 380515

Leicester CDA
30 New Walk
Leicester
0533 554464

Northamptonshire CDA
21-29 Hazelwood Road
Northampton
0604 24040

Nottinghamshire CDA
Dunkirk Road
Dunkirk
Nottingham
0602 705700

North

Ashington Community Initiatives Centre
Station Villas
Kenilworth Road
Ashington
Northumberland
0670 853619

Bradford Alternative Technology Centre
4 Grove Terrace
Bradford
Yorkshire
0274 394083

Cleveland Co-operative Agency
10A Albert Road
Middlesbrough
Cleveland
0642 210224

City of Manchester CDA
12 Mosley Street
Manchester
061 236 1274

Greater Manchester CDA
Holyoake House
Hanover Street
Manchester
061 833 9496

Merseyside CDA
Merseyside Unemployed Resource
Centre
24 Hardman Street
Liverpool
051 709 4363

North Region CDA
Bolbec Hall
Westgate Road
Newcastle-upon-Tyne
0632 610140

North Staffs CDA
Town Hall
Stoke-on-Trent
0782 48241 x 201

Sheffield Co-operative Development Group
Palatine Chambers
Pinston Street
Sheffield
0742 734563

York Co-ops Group
Box No 9
73 Walmgate
York

Antur Teifi
Graig Chambers
Newcastle Emlyn
Dyfed
0239 710238

Gwent Common Ownership Association
78 Bridge Street
Newport
Gwent
0633 51868

South Wales CDA
5 Mount Stuart Square
Cardiff
0222 494411

Wales Co-operative Development and Training Centre
55 Charles Street
Cardiff
0222 372237

West Glamorgan Common Ownership Development Agency
3 Christina Street
Swansea
0792 53498

Wales

Afan CDA
2nd Floor
Royal Buildings
Talbot Road
Port Talbot
West Glamorgan
0639 895173

Useful organisations

Beechwood College
Elmete Lane
Roundhay
Leeds
0532 720205

Co-operative Bank
PO Box 101
1 Balloon Street
Manchester
061 832 3456

Co-operative College
Stanford Hall
Loughborough
Leicester
050 982 2333

**Co-operative Development
Agency (national)**
20 Albert Embankment
London SE1
01 211 3351

Co-operative Research Unit
Systems Group
Open University
Walton Hall
Milton Keynes

Co-operative Union
Holyoake House
Hanover Street
Manchester
061 832 4300

**Industrial Common Ownership
Finance (ICOF)**
4 Saint Giles Street
Northampton
0604 37563

**Industrial Common Ownership
Movement (ICOM)**
7-8 The Corn Exchange
Leeds
0532 461737

ICOM North
2 Jesmond Road
Newcastle-upon-Tyne
0632 816632

London ICOM
7 Bradbury Street
London N16

Job Ownership Ltd
9 Poland Street
London W1
01 437 5511

**Plunkett Foundation for Co-
operative Studies**
31 Saint Giles
Oxford
0865 53960

Registrar of Friendly Societies
17 North Audley Street
London W1
01 629 7001

Scotland

**Scottish Co-operatives
Development Committee**
Templeton Business Centre
Templeton Street
Bridgeton
Glasgow
041 554 3797

Northern Ireland

**Co-operative Development
Agency — Belfast**
c/o Ulster People's College
30 Adelaide Park
Belfast
0232 665368

**Local Enterprise Development
Unit (LEDU)**
The Small Business Agency for
Northern Ireland
17-19 Linenhall Street
Belfast
0232 242582